*an intensive course in English*

---

## ENGLISH PRONUNCIATION

---

*exercises in SOUND SEGMENTS INTONATION, AND RHYTHM*

ENGLISH LANGUAGE INSTITUTE STAFF

**Robert Lado** and **Charles C. Fries**

ANN ARBOR | The University of Michigan Press

# TABLE OF CONTENTS

# PREFACE

The Lessons in Pronunciation contained in this book are part of the 1953 revision of An Intensive Course in English for Latin-American Students by the English Language Institute of the University of Michigan. They incorporate the results of approximately 12 years of experience teaching English to some 5000 Latin-American students. In this teaching the measurement of the effectiveness of the materials and the methods was always the practical one of understanding the flow of speech in an English speaking community and of being easily understood in such a community. The very existence of the English Language Institute depended upon the success of the teaching in enabling native speakers of Spanish and Portuguese with little or no command of English to live in the United States and to study and investigate in our medical schools, clinics, graduate schools, and research centers. For the acquisition of a practical understanding and use of English only a limited time was available and only those materials and methods that proved themselves essential and efficient could be retained for this course. The 1953 revision represents thus the lesson materials that have survived this continuing critical process in the hands of a number of different teachers.

Basically the materials rest upon a descriptive analysis of the English sound system carefully compared and contrasted with the sound systems of Spanish and Portuguese.[1] For this basic work Professor Kenneth L. Pike is largely responsible. Some of these background materials have now been published in separate books such as, for example, his Intonation of American English, and his Phonemics. He has however, continued to contribute his criticism and suggestions in our struggle with the practical teaching problems of the Intensive Course. Many of the teachers who have dealt with our materials have given much to make them effective. The work of the English Language Institute has been a truly cooperative enterprise by a devoted and generous staff. Some names need special mention, Dr. Robert Lado - who also contributed the drawings, Gerald Dykstra, Lois McIntosh, Eunice Pike, Ethel Wallis, Charles Michalski, Robert Maston, Gloria Goldenberg - who has taken such a personal interest in the production of the book in its present format. But the chief burden of directing the teaching of pronunciation, of gathering and sifting and utilizing the experience of the staff, and of writing the lessons that appear here has been carried by Dr. Betty Wallace Robinett.

Charles C. Fries

---

[1]In these particular lessons the special features of Portuguese are not included.

i

# INTRODUCTION

## Why teach pronunciation?

When a student of a foreign language who has had some instruction according to the usual methods first hears the spoken language he often fails to understand what has been said. He usually claims that the vocabulary of the utterance is too difficult for him. When a written text is placed before him he can, many times, interpret the same material correctly and react accordingly. It is not, then, only a lack of knowledge of vocabulary items which is causing the trouble. It is the inability of the student to recognize the sounds of the language.

For example, when a Spanish-speaking student learning English is confronted with a picture of a woman washing a baby and another in which the woman is watching a baby, he understands the difference in the two situations. But when he hears the English sentence The mother is watching the baby, he is often unable to decide which of the two actions is being described. Why? Because his decision usually depends upon the ability to differentiate between the final sounds of wash and watch, sounds which are extremely difficult for Latin-American students to distinguish because this contrast is not used in Spanish to distinguish meaning.

With the development of linguistic science has come the realization that the sounds of a language operate in a system. We must teach this sound system just as we teach the system of structure. Many words are distinguished solely by a difference of vowel sound as in peal, pill, pale, pal, pool, pull, pole, Paul. Likewise there are many words that are differentiated by a single consonant sound as in the series fin, pin, bin, tin, din, kin, sin, shin, thin. These contrasts in sound must be taught just as we teach the contrasting structures He's a doctor and Is he a doctor, pronounced with the same falling intonation.

## The Phonemic Alphabet

In teaching English pronunciation we soon see that there is very little help that we can get from the spelling of the words. Through, cough, hiccough, though reveal four different pronunciations for the one spelling ough. On the other hand, need, read, believe, machine, receive, we, people, key, contain eight different spellings for the vowel sound in the word need. Thus we are soon aware that English is not well spelled, i.e., there is not a one-to-one correspondence between the sounds as they are uttered and the letter or symbol which appears in the written word. What does this mean to a student who is trying to learn English as a foreign language? At first many students try to pronounce the word as it is spelled. They often try to pronounce the c of muscles or the e in table. It is necessary, therefore, to have some consistent representation of the language so that the student can have a clearer understanding of the distinctive sounds which exist in the language.

It is from the realization that the sounds of a language can be systematically described and represented that the phonemic alphabet has developed. A phonemic alphabet is a systematic representation of the distinctive sound units as they are found in meaningful contrast with each other in the language. Thus [p] is contrasted with [b] as shown by such words as pin and bin; [t] contrasted with [d] in time and dime. This alphabet then contains one symbol for each significant sound, and each sound which produces a contrast in meaning is represented by a particular symbol. Therefore in the previously mentioned series of words fin, pin, bin, tin, din, kin, sin, shin, thin, each distinctive consonant sound is represented by a different symbol. It is this principle of contrast which is important in teaching the distinctive sounds within a language, and the use of a phonemic alphabet is valuable in teaching these sounds. The alphabet on p. vii which we call the "special alphabet," is a phonemic representation of the sounds of English. It symbolizes only those differences in sound which produce a contrast in meaning, and it contains only a few symbols which are different from the ordinary letters of the spelling alphabet.

It should be emphasized here that the alphabet is not an end in itself. It is only a means to an end. Through its use the teacher can help the student fix in his mind these minimal differences of sound. This does not mean that when the student sees the symbol [ɪ], for the vowel sound of fill for example, that he will immediately know how to pronounce that sound. From the symbol alone, it would be impossible to know what the sound is. The sounds must be taught as sounds, never as symbols. It only means that when the student sees that particular symbol he knows that the sound it represents is different from that represented by [i], which is the vowel sound of feel. The symbol thereby becomes a memory clue for the student and helps him to make the distinction between feel and fill.

It is also necessary to symbolize the significant intonation sequences which occur within the language. This symbolization helps the student remember the intonation of English which he hears orally in class.

## The Introductory Lesson

The symbolization, in fact, has been found to be of such importance in the English Language Institute that the entire first day (four hours of class) in the Intensive Course is devoted to familiarizing the student with this symbolization so that the teachers may make maximum use of it throughout the course.

It was for this reason that the Introductory Lesson was devised. This lesson is divided into four parts, each part requiring about one hour of classroom practice. Part I is a general introduction to the phonemic alphabet and the intonation markings. Part II gives special attention to the symbols in the alphabet which are unfamiliar to the student. Part III is a series of drills on rhythm and intonation as represented by the intonation markings. Part IV attempts to give the student actual practice in using the symbolization in learning short conversations. It has been found that the use of this Introductory Lesson has materially improved the student's progress in learning the language.

## Exercises for recognition and production of sounds

Teaching the pronunciation of a foreign language has often meant teaching the students merely to produce the sounds of the language. But pronunciation of a foreign language is a two-fold process. It involves aural receptivity or the recognition of sounds as well as the actual production of sounds. That is, a student is faced with the problem of recognizing the significant sounds in the language he is learning before he can learn to produce them. Exercises for recognition are a regular part of the pronunciation lessons of this textbook. These exercises consist of pairs of words with minimal sound differences. The use of such exercises facilitates the recognition of these contrasts in sound. Such minimal pairs as man, men or bad, bed can be used to enable the student to hear the two significant sounds in English which we symbolize as [æ] and [ɛ].

A very simple drill for practicing the recognition of this and other distinctive differences can be made by arranging minimal pairs of words on the blackboard in columns thus:

| 1 [æ] | 2 [ɛ] |
|-------|-------|
| [mæn] | [mɛn] |
| [læs] | [lɛs] |
| [læd] | [lɛd] |
| [pæn] | [pɛn] |
| [bæt] | [bɛt] |
| [sæt] | [sɛt] |

The teacher pronounces pairs of words in order to make the student aware of the contrast.[1] When the teacher is certain that the students are beginning to hear these distinctions he can then have them actively participate in the exercise. As the teacher pronounces a word from these lists the student identifies it by giving the column number in which that word appears. This gives the student specific practice in recognizing the differences, a step which is necessary before he can produce the differences accurately.

The same type of exercise can be set up with sentences as well as words. Such a pair of sentences as The man built the house, The men built the house can be numbered and contrasted in the same way. These exercises can be varied by having a student go to the blackboard and point to the word or sentence instead of calling out the number as the teacher pronounces it. The students can also write down the number of the word or sentence as the teacher gives it.

Commencing in this way with aural perception or recognition of these distinctive contrasts the students are ready for oral production, the second part of the two-fold pronunciation process. The same exercises which were used for recognition can be used to teach production. The students can first pronounce in imitation of the teacher all of the words in one column and then those of the other. Secondly, the two sounds need to be contrasted by having the student pronounce a pair of words such as pan, pen to discover whether or not they can produce a clear distinction between the sounds. After the student has demonstrated his ability to make this contrast he can then select an isolated word from the lists, pronounce it, and have the teacher or another student identify it. This exercise can be carried on around the class as a series of production and recognition drills for each student, with one student pronouncing the word and his neighbor identifying it.

Another drill can be devised by having one student pronounce a word from the columns on the blackboard, and requiring the next student to pronounce the opposite word of the pair. This results in a recognition and production exercise for each student. These drills can be varied further by using the techniques described above for recognition exercises.

---

[1] Care must be taken to pronounce such contrasts with the same intonation on both words so that the sole difference between the words will be the sound under study.

## Aids to accurate production of sounds

There are in general three means of teaching specific sound segments: 1) by imitation, 2) by articulatory description, and 3) by comparison with the nearest sound in the student's native language.

Imitation of the teacher's pronunciation is the first step for the student, but imitation is usually not sufficient. Certain devices to illustrate the general position of the tongue in articulating sounds can help the students in attaining accuracy of pronunciation. Visual aids such as diagrams and charts provide a more vivid means of explanation. These diagrams seem to give the student a better grasp of the manner of production of these sounds than any number of descriptive paragraphs. The particular type of diagram which has been found helpful in teaching the pronunciation of English speech sounds is the simple face diagram. These will be found throughout the lessons.

Often by comparing and contrasting the English sound to the nearest sound in Spanish the Spanish-speaking student is able to improve his pronunciation. Therefore throughout the lessons there are footnotes to the teacher to call attention to these points of comparison and contrast. These contrasts can often be pointed out in the articulatory descriptions illustrated by the face diagrams.

The organization of the lessons is such that attention is centered not only on the contrastive sounds in English, but also on the sounds of English which may be confused with Spanish sounds. These lessons were prepared after a thorough analysis was made of the sound system of English and Spanish.

## Classroom atmosphere

Classroom atmosphere is especially important in classes dealing with pronunciation. Unless the student feels very much at home with his teacher and with his fellow students, he will not be able to achieve the freedom necessary for learning to produce sounds that are strange to him. Imitation of the teacher (even to an exaggerated degree at first) is essential in striving for an acceptable pronunciation of a foreign language. The student tends to be self-conscious if he is not completely at ease. If the classroom atmosphere is one of congeniality and freedom the student will find it easier to imitate and exaggerate the sounds which seem peculiar to him. Strain or an ill-at-ease feeling prevents development of the flexibility which is essential in learning new patterns of sound and structure.

Individual differences must also be considered in connection with imitative ability. To hold all students responsible for the same standard is an impossibility in something as unpredictable as imitative ability. The teacher needs to discover the utmost capacity of each student in this regard and hold him responsible for that capacity. This will provide a goal for each individual which will not be beyond his reach.

Over-correction may discourage the student and interruption of recitation sometimes disturbs him. It is better therefore to concentrate on the correction of a limited number of items at a time until the student can master them, and then add more until he finally reaches a state of satisfactory production in the whole utterance. It is better also to wait until the student has finished his utterance, then correct it and ask him to repeat it. In some cases a few words of encouragement prove an effective stimulus even though the student has not achieved the accuracy the teacher might desire.

## Specific Aims of Lessons I-X

The specific aims in the first ten lessons of this volume are four in number: 1) to enable the student to distinguish significant features of the sound system in English; 2) to enable the student to produce all significant vowel contrasts and the [r] sound satisfactorily; 3) to enable the student to use the 2-4 intonation curve in all utterances; and 4) to reinforce certain items of grammar which may present a problem in pronunciation.

Pronunciation is an oral process. Therefore it is well to remember that the progress of a student is in direct proportion to the amount of his actual practice in hearing and producing the language. With this approach in mind and with the systematic use of the recognition and production materials in this volume, the student will soon learn to comprehend the language more easily and speak it more accurately.

## Specific Aims of Lessons XI-XX

The aims of lessons XI-XX are also four: 1) to enable students to produce all significant consonant contrasts satisfactorily, plus some purely phonetic (allophonic) features which are outstanding in contrast to Spanish, e.g. English [l]; 2) to enable the student to use the 3-2 and the 2 2-4 intonation curves in addition to the 2-4 intonation curve; 3) to enable the student to produce longer utterances with smooth sentence rhythm; and 4) to reinforce further items of grammar which may present a problem in pronunciation.

## Specific Aims of Lessons XXI-XXXV

One of the primary aims of lessons XXI-XXX is to enable the students to produce consonant clusters and combinations satisfactorily. Appearing in great abundance and with great frequency in English are such clusters as [st] study, [fr] friend, [čt] watched, [lpt] helped, etc. Students whose native language does not permit such clusters find great difficulty in producing them accurately and with facility. Moreover, they find it difficult in producing them accurately and with facility. Moreover, they find it difficult to hear these combinations clearly. A continued effort is made in these ten lessons, to enable students to produce significant vowel and consonant contrasts satisfactorily in longer and connected contexts. Maintenance of acceptable intonation and rhythm patterns in longer contexts is also emphasized here.

The last five lessons in this volume (Lessons XXXI-XXXV) contain reviews of the sound segments which, on the basis of our experience, students find most difficult to produce correctly and in which they persist in making errors. An attempt is also made in these last lessons to give the students practice in maintaining accurate production of the sounds, rhythm, and intonation of English in less controlled situations. That is, unrehearsed talks be given by the students on many subjects in order to find the persistent errors which the student has retained. The readings on such subjects as "Politics and Government," "Music in the United States," and "Religion in the United States" are included for the purpose of practice on intonation and rhythm. There is no limit to the amount of "free" conversation which can be elicited from the students on these topics thereby giving the instructor an opportunity to discover the errors which the students are continuing to make. It is felt that by the use of these exercises the student will be able to achieve in actual speaking situations an accuracy which will be retained outside of the classroom.

## Specific exercises and drills in Lessons XXI-XXXV

In lessons XXI-XXXV as in the earlier ones the use of minimal pairs of words or sentences in the exercises has been found most effective. Continued use of such minimal pairs as washed [wɔšt] and watched [wɔčt] facilitates the recognition and production of such clusters as [št] and [čt].

An exercise for enabling the student to recognize and distinguish differences which involve consonant clusters has been introduced in these lessons. Thus in such a pair of sentences as <u>the students understand the lessons</u>, <u>the student understands the lessons</u> the primary aim is for the student to distinguish between the form <u>student</u> as contrasted with <u>students</u> and the form <u>understand</u> in contrast to <u>understands</u>. Likewise, the repetition of these pairs of sentences enables the student to gain control of the production of such clusters as [nts] or [ndz].

This exercise can be used in the same manner as the minimal pairs of words and sentences were used in the other lessons, that is, they can be numbered and the students can be asked to identify them by number. For a more varied type of exercise, however, the student can be asked to supply a correlative sentence to the one which he hears. Thus if the teacher, in using the aforementioned pair of sentences, pronounces <u>the student understands the lessons</u>, the student can reply <u>he understands the lessons</u>. Or if the teacher says <u>the students understand the lessons</u> the student in turn can show that he has recognized the sentence correctly by saying <u>they understand the lessons</u>.

Various combinations of consonants which occur within phrases have been found to cause a problem for many students of English. Thus special drills, "flexibility exercises," have been introduced to enable the student to gain control of his tongue in producing the combinations of consonants such as [z-Θ] in <u>he's thinking</u>, [z-ð] in <u>where's the man,</u> [št-ð] in <u>washed the dress</u>, [st-l] in <u>the last list</u>, etc.

### Supplementary material

In lessons XXI-XXXV some supplementary information concerning English is presented to the students. These items have been found necessary for foreign students attempting to understand and use English. One such item is a discussion of dialectal and individual differences in pronunciation in the United States (Lesson XIX).

Since English is not always spelled in a manner consistent with its pronunciation the students need every possible aid to learning the pronunciation of words which they may see for the first time. In an attempt to help the students make use of the regularities of spelling which do exist in English, a list of the most common regularities in English vowel spelling is supplied (Lesson XXVI).

### Summary

Upon completion of the thirty-five lessons of pronunciation the student should have acquired a basic knowledge of the sound system in English, including intonation and rhythm patterns. Knowledge of the system, however, does not necessarily signify that the student can produce the sounds, intonation, and rhythm of English with complete accuracy. Actual practice on all the points of contrast in the system of English and also on those points which contrast with the native language of the student is continuously urged. By the use of the specific drills and exercises contained in all of these lessons the student will finally obtain freedom in the pronunciation of the language, that is, he will be able to produce the language accurately and with ease.

# THE SPECIAL ALPHABET[1]

## CONSONANTS

| | | | | | | | | | |
|---|---|---|---|---|---|---|---|---|---|
| [b] | [bi] | be | [p] | [pe] | pay | [ŋ] | [sɪŋ] | sing |
| [d] | [du] | do | [r] | [rum] | room | [Θ] | [Θɪŋk] | think |
| [f] | [fɔr] | four | [s] | [se] | say | [ð] | [ðe] | they |
| [g] | [go] | go | [t] | [taɪm] | time | [hw] | [hwət] | what |
| [h] | [hom] | home | [v] | [váuəl] | vowel | [š] | [ši] | she |
| [k] | [kəm] | come | [w] | [wi] | we | [ž] | [yúžuəl] | usual |
| [l] | [let] | late | [y] | [yu] | you | [č] | [čərč] | church |
| [m] | [mæn] | man | [z] | [zíro] | zero | [ǰ] | [ǰo] | Joe |
| [n] | [no] | no | | | | | | |

## VOWELS

| | | | | | | | | | |
|---|---|---|---|---|---|---|---|---|---|
| [i] | [it] | eat | [u] | [du] | do | [aɪ] | [aɪ] | I |
| [ɪ] | [ɪt] | it | [ʊ] | [gʊd] | good | [aʊ] | [naʊ] | now |
| [e] | [let] | late | [o] | [no] | no | [ɔɪ] | [bɔɪ] | boy |
| [ɛ] | [lɛt] | let | [ɔ] | [sɔ] | saw | | | |
| [æ] | [mæn] | man | | | | [ ´ ] | accent |
| [ə] | [bət] | but | | | | | | |
| [a] | [nat] | not | | | | | | |

---

[1]This is a simplified phonemic representation of the sounds of English.

# INTRODUCTORY LESSON

## PART I[1]

1. Three essentials of good pronunciation
2. The need for a special alphabet
3. The sounds of English.
4. The marking of intonation
5. Rhythm

### 1. Three essentials of good pronunciation

    a) The sounds of the language

    b) The intonation of the language

    c) The rhythm of the language

The sounds of the language are important. They differentiate words. Notice the following examples:

    think    sink        search    church        eat    it

Intonation is produced by the sequences of pitch (tone) of the voice. Each language has its characteristic sequences of pitch. Listen carefully to the intonation of English.

    He's coming.        the university        in the class

English rhythm is characterized by the regular recurrence of emphasized syllables. Listen carefully to the rhythm of English.

    answer        the class

    an answer        in grammar

    a good answer        is interesting

    The class    in grammar    is interesting.

### 2. The need for a special alphabet

A special alphabet is necessary in learning to pronounce English. There are more sounds in English than there are letters in the spelling alphabet.

a) The same spelling may have various pronunciations. Observe the different pronunciations of ough in the following words.

| | | | | | |
|---|---|---|---|---|---|
| bough | [aʊ] | although | [o] | cough | [ɔf] |
| through | [u] | bought | [ɔ] | hiccough | [əp] |
| | | | | enough | [əf] |

---

[1] Each of the four separate parts of the Introductory Lesson requires about one hour of class work.

**b)** The same sound may have various spellings. Notice the different spellings of the sound [i] in the following words.

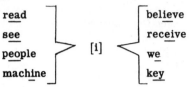

| read | | believe |
|------|--|---------|
| see | | receive |
| people | [i] | we |
| machine | | key |

### 3. The sounds of English

**a)** Consonants

| 1. Sounds represented by familiar symbols[1] | | 2. Sounds represented by unfamiliar symbols |
|---|---|---|

| [b] | be | [p] | pay |
|-----|-----|-----|-----|
| [d] | do | [r] | room |
| [f] | four | [s] | say |
| [g] | go | [t] | time |
| [h] | home | [v] | vowel |
| [k] | come | [w] | we |
| [l] | late | [y] | you |
| [m] | man | [z] | zero |
| [n] | no | | |

| [ŋ] | sing |
|-----|------|
| [Θ] | think |
| [ð] | they |
| [hw][2] | what |
| [š] | she |
| [ž] | usual |
| [č] | church |
| [ǰ] | Joe |

---

[1] These symbols may be similar to those in many languages, but the sounds are usually somewhat different.

[2] Unfamiliar combination.

## b) Vowels [1]

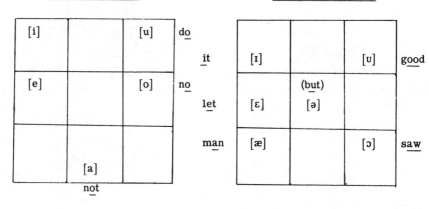

(1) Sounds represented by familiar symbols

eat   [i]       [u]   do

                      it

late  [e]       [o]   no

                      let

           [a]  man

           not

(2) Sounds represented by unfamiliar symbols

        [ɪ]        [ʊ]   good

            (but)
        [ɛ]  [ə]

        [æ]        [ɔ]   saw

### (3) Diphthongs

[aɪ] I        [aʊ] now        [ɔɪ] boy

### (4) Vowel Chart

|       | | | |       |
|-------|---|---|---|-------|
| eat   | [i] |     | [u] | Luke |
| it    | [ɪ] |     | [ʊ] | look |
| late  | [e] | (cut) | [o] | coat |
| let   | [ɛ] | [ə] |     |      |
| cat   | [æ] |     | [ɔ] | caught |
|       |     | [a] |     |      |
|       |     | cot |     |      |

[aɪ]        [aʊ]        [ɔɪ]
buy         bough       boy

---

[1] Note to the teacher: Exaggerate the length of the vowels and point out the diphthongization of [e] and [o].

## 4. The marking of intonation

A line represents the relative pitch (tone) of the voice.

a) A vertical line represents a change in pitch between syllables.

[ðə sɪmbəl]                [aɪ no ðə sɪmbəl]

[ðə nəmbər]                [aɪ no ðə nəmbər]

[ðə lɛtər]                [aɪ no ðə lɛtər]

[ðə yunɪvərsɪti]                [aɪ no ðə yunɪvərsɪti]

b) A diagonal line represents a change in pitch on the vowel sound. The vowel sound is prolonged.

[ðə klæs]                [aɪ si ðə klæs]

[ðə nem]                [aɪ si ðə nem]

[ðə wərd]                [aɪ si ðə wərd]

[ðə rum]                [aɪ si ðə rum]

## 5. Rhythm

Notice the regular recurrence of emphasized syllables in the following groups of words and sentences.

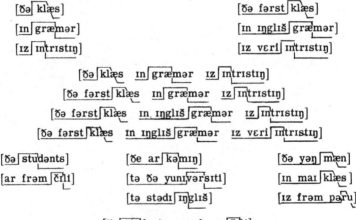

[ðə klæs]                [ðə fərst klæs]

[ɪn græmər]                [ɪn ɪŋglɪš græmər]

[ɪz ɪntrɪstɪŋ]                [ɪz vɛri ɪntrɪstɪŋ]

[ðə klæs ɪn græmər ɪz ɪntrɪstɪŋ]

[ðə fərst klæs ɪn græmər ɪz ɪntrɪstɪŋ]

[ðə fərst klæs ɪn ɪŋglɪš græmər ɪz ɪntrɪstɪŋ]

[ðə fərst klæs ɪn ɪŋglɪš græmər ɪz vɛri ɪntrɪstɪŋ]

[ðə studənts]    [ðe ar kəmɪŋ]    [ðə yəŋ mæn]

[ar frəm čɪli]    [tə ðə yunɪvərsɪti]    [ɪn maɪ klæs]

[tə stədɪ ɪŋglɪš]    [ɪz frəm pəru]

[ðə studənts ar frəm čɪli]

[ðe ar kəmɪŋ tə ðə yunɪvərsɪti tə stədɪ ɪŋglɪš]

[ðə yəŋ mæn ɪn maɪ klæs ɪz frəm pəru]

# INTRODUCTORY LESSON

## PART II

1. Familiar symbols
2. Drill on especially difficult consonant symbols
3. Hearing vowel contrasts
4. Practice with all the symbols

### 1. Familiar symbols[1]

| | | | |
|---|---|---|---|
| 1. [b] | 6. [k] | 10. [p] | 14. [v] |
| 2. [d] | 7. [l] | 11. [r] | 15. [w] |
| 3. [f] | 8. [m] | 12. [s] | 16. [y] |
| 4. [g] | 9. [n] | 13. [t] | 17. [z] |
| 5. [h] | | | |

Identify by number the consonant sound the teacher substitutes for the underlined sound in the lists below.

Examples:

| [bit] (1) | [det] (2) | [su] (12) | [kot] (6) |
|---|---|---|---|
| [bit] | [let] | [tu] | [rot] |
| [fit] | [pet] | [su] | [not] |
| [hit] | [wet] | [yu] | [vot] |
| [mit] | [get] | [zu] | [mot] |
| [hit] | [ket] | [du] | [got] |

---

[1] Note to the teacher: These symbols should be written on the blackboard. The purpose of this exercise is only to give the student confidence by showing that most of the symbols of the special alphabet are familiar to him. Only a few minutes should be devoted to this exercise in order to have the major part of the hour for practice with the unfamiliar symbols of the alphabet.

## 2. Drill on especially difficult consonant symbols

Identify by number the sound in the word which the teacher pronounces.

| 1 [d] | 2 [Θ] | 1 [t] | 2 [ð] | 1 [h] | 2 [w] |
|---|---|---|---|---|---|
| [dæŋk] | [Θæŋk] | [to] | [ðo] | [het] | [wet] |
| [daɪ] | [Θaɪ] | [tɛn] | [ðɛn] | [hərd] | [wərd] |
| [fed] | [feΘ] | [tɛr] | [ðɛr] | [haɪr] | [waɪr] |
| [bæd] | [bæΘ] | [tiz] | [ðiz] | [hip] | [wip] |
| [dəm] | [Θəm] | [toz] | [ðoz] | [hɪt] | [wɪt] |
| [dɪn] | [Θɪn] | [tæn] | [ðæn] | [hez] | [wez] |

| 1 [ŋ] | 2 [m] | 1 [ǰ] | 2 [s] | 1 [č] | 2 [z] |
|---|---|---|---|---|---|
| [səŋ] | [səm] | [ǰuz] | [suz] | [ču] | [zu] |
| [rəŋ] | [rəm] | [ǰip] | [sip] | [čɪp] | [zɪp] |
| [rɪŋ] | [rɪm] | [ǰɪn] | [sɪn] | [hæč] | [hæz] |
| [ræŋ] | [ræm] | [ǰo] | [so] | [kauč] | [kauz] |
| [sæŋ] | [sæm] | [ǰel] | [sel] | [ič] | [iz] |
| [hæŋ] | [hæm] | [ǰok] | [sok] | [ɪč] | [ɪz] |

| 1 [ž] | 2 [s] | | 1 [š] | 2 [z] |
|---|---|---|---|---|
| [bež] | [bes] | | [šu] | [zu] |
| [ruž] | [rus] | | [šɪp] | [zɪp] |
| [mɛžər] | [mes] | | [ši] | [zi] |
| [ližər] | [lisər] | | [hæš] | [hæz] |

| 1 [š] | 2 [ǰ] | | 1 [ž] | 2 [č] |
|---|---|---|---|---|
| [šuz] | [ǰuz] | | [ruž] | [rɪč] |
| [šip] | [ǰip] | | [bež] | [bɪč] |
| [šed] | [ǰed] | | [mɛžər] | [məč] |
| [šo] | [ǰo] | | [plɛžər] | [tičər] |

## 3. Hearing vowel contrasts[1]

Identify by number the vowel sound the teacher substitutes for the underlined sound.

Familiar Symbols                              Unfamiliar Symbols

| 1 | [i] |     | [u] | 6 |
|---|-----|-----|-----|---|
| 2 | [e] |     | [o] | 7 |
|   |     | (4)<br>[a] |   |   |

3  [aɪ]   5  [au]

| 1 | [ɪ] |     | [ʊ] | 5 |
|---|-----|-----|-----|---|
| 2 | [ɛ] | (4)<br>[ə] |   |   |
| 3 | [æ] |     | [ɔ] | 6 |

[ɔɪ]   7

Examples:                                    Examples:

[r<u>i</u>d]   (1)        [tul]   (6)        [l<u>ɪ</u>d]   (1)        [læst]   (3)

[rid]    [til]                              [lɪrd]    [lɪst]
[rad]    [tol]                              [læd]     [lɛst]
[rud]    [tel]                              [lɛd]     [lɔst]
[rod]    [tul]                              [lɔd]     [ləst]

[list]   [bit]    [tik]                     [tɛl]     [lʊk]
[lust]   [bot]    [tek]                     [tɔl]     [lɪk]
[lest]   [but]                              [tɔɪl]    [lək]
         [bet]                              [trl]     [læk]
         [baɪt]
         [baut]                   [bɪt]    [tʊk]    [kəd]
                                  [bæt]    [tɔk]    [kɪd]
                                  [bɛt]    [tæk]    [kæd]
                                  [bɔt]    [tək]    [kʊd]
                                  [bət]    [tɪk]    [kɔd]

---

[1] Note to the teacher: Spend as little time as possible with familiar vowel symbols in order to devote the maximum of time and practice to the unfamiliar vowel symbols.

## 4. Practice with all the symbols[1]

Pronounce the following words.

| I | II | III |
|---|----|-----|
| 1. [mit] | 21. [sɛz] | 41. [ðɪs] |
| 2. [hat] | 22. [mɪlk] | 42. [lɪv] |
| 3. [pliz] | 23. [hɛlp] | 43. [bɔɪ] |
| 4. [se] | 24. [baɪ] | 44. [šo] |
| 5. [fálo] | 25. [tébəl] | 45. [kaʊ] |
| 6. [tek] | 26. [sárí] | 46. [stə́di] |
| 7. [nat] | 27. [bʊk] | 47. [ǰok] |
| 8. [let] | 28. [aʊt] | 48. [wɪð] |
| 9. [si] | 29. [mæn] | 49. [klæs] |
| 10. [ar] | 30. [smaɪl] | 50. [tič] |
| 11. [it] | 31. [æt] | 51. [ɪz] |
| 12. [lat] | 32. [gɛt] | 52. [sən] |
| 13. [sin] | 33. [hænd] | 53. [Θæŋk] |
| 14. [pe] | 34. [sɪt] | 54. [šek] |
| 15. [plet] | 35. [kəp] | 55. [wən] |
| 16. [spik] | 36. [dɔg] | 56. [stæmp] |
| 17. [milz] | 37. [spɛnd] | 57. [čɛk] |
| 18. [du] | 38. [hæt] | 58. [əs] |
| 19. [yu] | 39. [ɪt] | 59. [məč] |
| **20.** [raɪt] | 40. [vížən] | 60. [mɪs] |

---

[1] Note to the teacher: These words can be presented on flash cards or on the blackboard. Column III will require more practice than columns I and II because it contains more of the unfamiliar symbols.

## PART III

1. The emphasized syllable is loud
2. The emphasized syllable is long
3. The emphasized syllable has the intonation curve
4. The same marking indicates rhythm and intonation
5. Practice with intonation and rhythm markings
6. Exercise in reading

### 1. The emphasized syllable is loud

[nəmˈbər]　　　　　[ðə ˈnəmbər]　　　　　[ə ˈnəmbər]

[nəm] is stressed or emphasized. Each word of more than one syllable has one syllable that is pronounced louder than the others.

Pronounce the following:

| [stuˈdənt] | [spæˈnɪš] | [ðə ˈnəmbər] | [ə ˈnəmbər] |
| [ˈgræmər] | [spɛˈlɪŋ] | [ðə ˈspɛlɪŋ] | [ə ˈsɪmbəl] |
| [ˈstədi] | [ˈɪŋglɪš] | [ðə ˈsɪmbəl] | |

### 2. The emphasized syllable is long

[ˈælfəbɛt]　　　　　[ən ˈælfəbɛt]

[æl] is long. It is the emphasized syllable and is longer than the others.

Pronounce the following:

| [ˈgræǰuət] | [ðə ˈgræǰuət] | [ə ˈgræǰuət] |
| [ˈyɛstərdi] | | |
| [yunɪˈvərsɪti] | [ðə yunɪˈvərsɪti] | [ə yunɪˈvərsɪti] |
| [ˈɪntrɪstɪŋ] | | |

### 3. The emphasized syllable has the intonation curve

[ɛgˈzæmpəl]

[zæm] is high in contrast with [ɛg] and [pəl]. It is the emphasized syllable.

[fəˈnɛtɪk]　　　　　[kənˈsɪstənt]

### 4. The same marking indicates rhythm and intonation

The same line 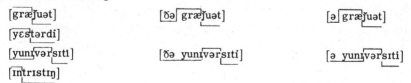 indicates rhythm and intonation. The high part of the line indicates the emphasized syllable and high intonation.

Exercise: Read the examples in Sections 1, 2 and 3. Use the rhythm and intonation marked.

5. Practice with intonation and rhythm markings

(a) Pronounce these series of examples in imitation of the teacher.

[rum]            [maɪ rum]            [ðə rum]
[nem]            [maɪ nem]            [ðə nem]
[fon]            [maɪ fon]            [ðə fon]
[wərd]           [maɪ wərd]           [ðə wərd]
[klæs]           [maɪ klæs]           [ðə klæs]

[aɪm frəm kyubə]              [aɪm frəm pænəma]
[aɪm frəm čɪli]               [aɪm frəm mɛksɪko]
[aɪm frəm ɪŋglənd]            [aɪm frəm kələmbɪə]
[aɪm frəm čaɪnə]             [aɪm frəm jərməni]

[aɪ lɪv ɪn kələmbɪə]          [aɪ lɪv ɪn kyubə]
[aɪ lɪv ɪn bəlɪvɪə]          [aɪ lɪv ɪn čɪli]
[aɪ lɪv ɪn mɛksɪko]          [aɪ lɪv ɪn čaɪnə]
[aɪ lɪv ɪn pænəma]           [aɪ lɪv ɪn ɪŋglənd]

[əndərstænd]      [spik]        [rɪpit]        [lɪv]
[aɪ əndərstænd]   [aɪ spik]     [aɪ rɪpit]     [aɪ lɪv]
[yu əndərstænd]   [yu spik]     [yu rɪpit]     [yu lɪv]

[frəm kyubə]      [frəm brəzɪl]     [frəm mɛksɪko]
[frəm čɪli]       [frəm pəru]       [frəm pænəma]
[frəm ɪŋgənd]     [frəm nu yɔrk]    [frəm ɪtəli]
[frəm čaɪnə]      [frəm fræns]      [frəm jərmənɪ]
                  [frəm spen]
                  [frəm gris]

[ɪn kələmbɪə]     [ɪn gwatəmalə]    [ɪn brəzɪl]
[ɪn bəlɪvɪə]      [ɪn vɛnəzwelə]    [ɪn pəru]
[ɪn handʊrəs]     [ɪn nɪkəragwə]    [ɪn spen]
[ɪn kərakəs]      [ɪn arjəntinə]    [ɪn fræns]

[bɪgɪn]      [θɪŋk]      [kəm]      [stədi]
[aɪ bɪgɪn]   [aɪ θɪŋk]   [aɪ kəm]   [aɪ stədi]
[yu bɪgɪn]   [yu θɪŋk]   [yu kəm]   [yu stədi]

[wən]   [θrɨ]   [faɪv]   [et]    [tɛn]   [zɪro]
[tu]    [fɔr]   [sɪks]   [naɪn]          [sɛvən]

b) Read these examples.

6. Exercise in reading

   Read these groups of words with the intonation and rhythm marked.

1. [maɪ nem]              11. [frəm kərakəs]
2. [ðə spɛlɪŋ]            12. [aɪm frəm kyubə]
3. [ə sɪmbəl]            13. [aɪ lɪv ɪn spen]
4. [ɪn arʒəntinə]         14. [yu əndərstænd]
5. [aɪ stədi]            15. [wən sɪmbəl]
6. [frəm pænəma]         16. [ə fənɛtɪk ælfəbɛt]
7. [tɔk sloli]           17. [aɪ əraɪv]
8. [pliz rɪpɪt]          18. [aɪ dont əndərstænd]
9. [ðə saund]            19. [yu spik spænɪš]
10. [ɪn gwatəmalə]        20. [aɪ θɪŋk]

# INTRODUCTORY LESSON
## PART IV

1. Classroom phrases and conversation
2. Introduction
3. Introduction monologue

## 1. Classroom phrases and conversation

Pronounce the groups of words with uniform rhythm.

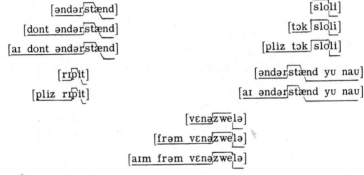

Conversation:[1]

Teacher: Where are you from?
Student: [aɪ dont əndərstænd]

Teacher: Where are you from?
Student: [pliz tɔk sloli]

Teacher: Where are you from?
Student: [pliz rɪpit]

Teacher: Where are you from?
Student: [aɪ əndərstænd yu nau aɪm frəm vɛnəzwelə]

---

[1] Note to the teacher: In the conversations in this part of the lesson, only sentences written in the special alphabet should be pronounced by the students. The questions, written in traditional orthography, are to be given by the teacher.

## 2. Introduction

Pronounce the groups of words with uniform rhythm.

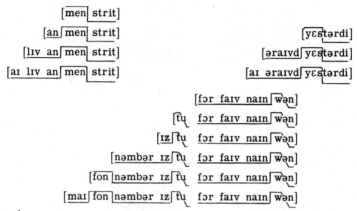

Conversation:[1]

Teacher: What is your name?

Student: [maɪ nem ɪz hwan ˈpɛrɛz]

Teacher: Where are you from?

Student: [aɪm frəm vɛnəzwelə]

Teacher: Where do you live?

Student: [aɪ lɪv an ˈmen strit]

Teacher: What is your phone number?

Student: [maɪ fon nəmbər ɪz ˈtu fɔr faɪv naɪn ˈwən]

Teacher: When did you arrive?

Student: [aɪ əraɪvd ˈyɛstərdi]

---

[1] Note to the teacher: The students should first practice these conversations exactly as they are written. Then they can be asked to substitute their own name, address, and telephone number.

3. Introduction monologue[1]

Practice the following monologue.

[maɪ nem ɪz hwan pɛ́rɛz aɪm frəm vɛnəzwélə
aɪ lɪv an men strit maɪ fon nəmbər ɪz tu
fɔr faɪv naɪn wən aɪ əraɪvd yɛstərdi]

---

[1] Note to the teacher: Each student should first practice the monologue in connected sequence exactly as it is written. Then the student can substitute information about himself and pronounce the sentences in a connected sequence.

# LESSON I

## PRONUNCIATION

1. Hearing vowel contrasts
2. Pronunciation of THE, A, AN
3. Reduced forms of BE
4. Reduced forms of HE, SHE, WE, YOU
5. The sounds represented by the special alphabet

## 1. Hearing vowel contrasts

The teacher will pronounce the following words. Listen carefully and see if you can hear the difference in these sounds.

| | | | | | |
|---|---|---|---|---|---|
| 1. [mit] | 4. [mɛt] | 1. [kæt] | 1. [luk] | 1. [bot] | 1. [baɪ] |
| 2. [mɪt] | 5. [mæt] | 2. [kət] | 2. [lʊk] | 2. [bɔt] | 2. [baʊ] |
| 3. [met] | | 3. [kat] | 3. [lək] | 3. [bət] | 3. [bɔɪ] |

Notice the relative position of the vowel sounds in the mouth. The teacher will pronounce the English vowel sounds as numbered.

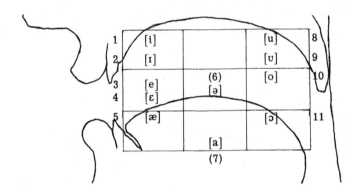

Identify the vowel sound in the following words by number as the teacher pronounces them. Pay attention only to the vowel sound.

| | | | |
|---|---|---|---|
| [mit] | [kæt] | [lʊk] | [bot] |
| [met] | [kət] | [lək] | [bɔt] |
| [mæt] | [kæt] | [luk] | [bət] |
| [mɛt] | [kat] | [lək] | [bɔt] |
| [mɪt] | [kət] | [lʊk] | [bot] |
| [mit] | [kæt] | [luk] | [bət] |

15

2. Pronunciation of THE, A, AN

Pronounce the following groups of words.

[ðə mæn]                          [ðɪ ɛgzæmpəl]

[ðə sɪmbəl]                       [ðɪ ækšən]

[ðə nem]                          [ðɪ ɪntrədəkšən]

[ðə wərd]                         [ðɪ ælfəbɛt]

[ðə saund]                        [ðɪ ɛksplanešən]

[ðə lɔŋ sɛntəns]                  [ðɪ ɪntrɪstɪŋ klæs]

[ðə nu lɛsən]                     [ðɪ ɛksələnt ɛgzæmpəl]

[ðə gud ænsər]                    [ðɪ izi buk]

[ðə nu buk]                       [ðɪ ərli klæs]

[ðə dɪfɪkəlt klæs]                [ðɪ ɪntrɪstɪŋ lɛsən]

Notice that the is pronounced [ðə] before words beginning with a consonant. It is pronounced [ðɪ] before words beginning with a vowel.

Exercise: Complete the following sentence with groups of words from the lists above.

[ðe si _____ ]              [ðe si ðə nəmbər]

Pronounce the following groups of words.

[ə mæn]                           [ə lɔŋ sɛntəns]

[ə sɪmbəl]                        [ə nu lɛsən]

[ə nem]                           [ə gud ænsər]

[ə wərd]                          [ə nu buk]

[ə saund]                         [ə dɪfɪkəlt klæs]

[ə nəmbər]                        [ə lɔŋ nem]

Notice that a, pronounced [ə], is used before a word beginning with a consonant sound.

Pronounce the following groups of words.

[ən ɛgzæmpəl]                     [ən ɪntrɪstɪŋ klæs]

[ən ækšən]                        [ən ɛksələnt ɛgzæmpəl]

[ən ɪntrədəkšən]                  [ən izi buk]

[ən ælfəbɛt]                      [ən ərli klæs]

[ən ɛksplanešən]                  [ən ɪntrɪstɪŋ lɛsən]

Notice that an, pronounced [ən], is used before a word beginning with a vowel sound.

Exercise: Complete the following sentence with groups of words from the lists above.

      [ðe si _____ ]              [ðe si ə⌐klæs]

                                   [ðe si ən ɛgzæmpəl]

## 3. Reduced forms of be

Observe the difference in the vowel sounds in the following two styles of speech.

| Slow Pronunciation | Rapid Pronunciation |
|---|---|
| [ðoz ar nu] | [ðoz ər nu] |
| [ðiz ar dífrənt] | [ðiz ər dífrənt] |

Notice that [ar] becomes [ər] in rapid pronunciation.

Observe the difference in the vowel sounds in the following sentences.

      [hi ɪz hə́ŋgri]                  [hiz hə́ŋgri]

      [ðe ar ə́rli]                    [ðɛr ə́rli]

Notice that the [ɪ] of [ɪz] is omitted in rapid pronunciation: [hi ɪz] is pronounced as one word--[hiz]. The [e] in [ðe] and the [a] in [ar] change to [ɛ]: [ðe ar] is pronounced as one word--[ðɛr].

The forms [ər], [hiz], and [ðɛr] are reduced forms.

Am, is and are are usually reduced in normal rapid pronunciation.

Pronounce the following sentences which contain reduced forms of be. Use the normal rapid pronunciation. Use the 2-4 intonation curve.

| | |
|---|---|
| [aɪm⌐taɪrd] | [ðə hæts⌐larʃ] |
| [yur⌐lɛt] | [ðɪ ænsərz⌐ɛksələnt] |
| [hiz⌐ərli] | [ðæts⌐ɪntrɪstɪŋ] |
| [ɪts⌐old] | [ðoz ər⌐nu] |
| [wɪr⌐bɪzi] | [ðiz ər⌐dɪfrənt] |
| [ðɛr⌐ʃɔrt] | [ðiz ər⌐ɪzi] |
| [ðə rumz⌐plɛzənt] | [ðɛrz⌐ʃan] |
| [ðə gərlz⌐yəŋ] | [šiz ə⌐nərs] |
| [ðə suts⌐braun] | [huz ðə⌐tičər] |

## 4. Reduced forms of HE, SHE, WE, YOU

He, she, we, and you are frequently reduced in normal rapid conversation.

|  | Full form | Reduced form |
|---|---|---|
| he | [hi] | [i] |
| she | [ši] | [šɪ] |
| we | [wi] | [wɪ] |
| you | [yu] | [yʊ] or [yə] |

Pronounce the following sentences with normal rapid pronunciation. Observe the reduced forms of he, she, we, and you. Mimic the intonation of the teacher.

[ɪz i ə student]

[hwɛr ɪz i]

[ɪz šɪ ə nərs]

[ar wɪ let]

Read the following sentences with normal rapid pronunciation. Mimic the intonation of the teacher.

[ar wɪ ərli]              [yʊ stədi]

[ar yə let]               [wɪ notɪs ɪt]

[ɪz i hɪr]                [hu ɪz i]

[hwɛr ɪz i]             [wɪ lərn ɪt]

[ɪz šɪ bɪzi]           [šɪ əndərstænds ɪt]

[hwɛr ar wɪ]          [ar yu ə tičər]

[šɪ frikwəntli smaɪlz]    [šɪ spiks ɪŋglɪš]

[hwət ɪz i]            [wɪ laɪk aɪs krim]

[hwət ar yʊ]          [ar yu bɪzi]

Practice the following conversation:

Student A. [ɪz i ə student]

Student B. [yɛs i ɪz]

Continue the exercise substituting you, she, we in the question.

## 5. The sounds represented by the alphabet:  consonant sounds

Listen to the teacher read the following words. Notice especially the consonant sound that precedes each group of words. Pronounce the words after him.[1]

| | | | | |
|---|---|---|---|---|
| [p] | [pe] | pay | [prédɪkət] | predicate |
| | [paɪp] | pipe | [pəzíšən] | position |
| [b] | [bi] | be | [brəzíl] | Brazil |
| | [bʊk] | book | [byútɪfəl] | beautiful |
| [t] | [taɪm] | time | [fənétɪks] | phonetics |
| | [tíčər] | teacher | [stə́di] | study |
| [d] | [du] | do | [dέfɪnɪt] | definite |
| | [aɪdíə] | idea | [əndərstǽnd] | understand |
| [k] | [kaʊ] | cow | [kágnet] | cognate |
| | [kəm] | come | [kə́stəm] | custom |
| [g] | [go] | go | [santɪágo] | Santiago |
| | [bɪgín] | begin | [ɛgzǽmpəl] | example |
| [f] | [fes] | face | [fríkwəntlɪ] | frequently |
| | [fálo] | follow | [dífɪkəlt] | difficult |
| [v] | [váʊəl] | vowel | [ɪnvέrɪəbəl] | invariable |
| | [vərb] | verb | [ǽǰɛktɪv] | adjective |
| [Ɵ] | [Ɵɪŋk] | think | [Ɵə́rsti] | thirsty |
| | [nɔrƟ] | north | [saʊƟ] | south |

---

[1]Note to the teacher: The teacher should pronounce words in lists with a falling, not a rising pitch. Students should be encouraged to do likewise in their mimicry of the teacher's pronunciation.

It is important from the very beginning to start training the students in the simplest pattern of pitch and stress which will be satisfactory in conversation. If pitch and stress are correct, slight errors in sound will not be so prominent. One of the most es - sential patterns is the English high-to-low pitch at the ends of sentences--on final phrases, on final words of several syllables, or on final words of one syllable in which the pitch slurs downward on a vowel. This pattern is one that needs particular drill for Spanish-speaking students.

| [ð] | [ðe]        | they      | [ðæt]          | that         |
|     | [ðə mæn]    | the man   | [əðər]         | other        |
| [s] | [se]        | say       | [spǽnɪš]       | Spanish      |
|     | [spɛ́lɪŋ]    | spelling  | [sɛ́ntəns]      | sentence     |
| [z] | [zíro]      | zero      | [saundz]       | sounds       |
|     | [brəzíl]    | Brazil    | [ɛ́ksərsaɪz]    | exercise     |
| [š] | [ši]        | she       | [kənstrə́kšən]  | construction |
|     | [dɪktéšən]  | dictation | [spǽnɪš]       | Spanish      |
| [ž] | [mɛ́žər]     | measure   | [vížən]        | vision       |
|     | [plɛ́žər]    | pleasure  | [ruž]          | rouge        |
| [h] | [hi]        | he        | [hɛlp]         | help         |
|     | [hə́ŋgri]    | hungry    | [hu]           | who          |
| [m] | [mæn]       | man       | [bátəm]        | bottom       |
|     | [mísɪz]     | Mrs.      | [rɪzɛ́mbəl]     | resemble     |
| [n] | [no]        | no        | [lɛ́sən]        | lesson       |
|     | [mɛ́ni]      | many      | [ɪn]           | in           |
| [ŋ] | [sɪŋ]       | sing      | [síŋgyələr]    | singular     |
|     | [lɔŋ]       | long      | [hə́ŋgri]       | hungry       |
| [l] | [let]       | late      | [lərn]         | learn        |
|     | [klæs]      | class     | [ártɪkəl]      | article      |
| [r] | [rid]       | read      | [tíčər]        | teacher      |
|     | [wərdz]     | words     | [órdər]        | order        |
| [w] | [wi]        | we        | [wərd]         | word         |
|     | [wən]       | one       | [vɛnəzwélən]   | Venezuelan   |
| [y] | [yu]        | you       | [yúrəp]        | Europe       |
|     | [yuz]       | use       | [brəzílyən]    | Brazilian    |
| [hw]| [hwaɪ]      | why       | [hwaɪt]        | white        |
|     | [hwɛn]      | when      | [hwɪč]         | which        |

| [č] | [čərč] | church | [čímni] | chimney |
| | [čɪlí] | Chile | [čóklət] | chocolate |
| [ǰ] | [ǰok] | joke | [sə́bǰɪkt] | subject |
| | [ríǰɪd] | rigid | [larǰ] | large |

The sounds represented by the special alphabet: vowel sounds

| [i] | [it] | eat | [ízi] | easy |
| | [spíkər] | speaker | [kóstə ríkə] | Costa Rica |
| [ɪ] | [ɪz] | is | [ɪmpórtənt] | important |
| | [íŋglɪš] | English | [vérɪ] | very |
| [e] | [se] | say | [ðe] | they |
| | [ɛksplén] | explain | [índɪket] | indicate |
| [ɛ] | [sɛz] | says | [ɛksplén] | explain |
| | [éndɪŋz] | endings | [létər] | letter |
| [æ] | [æd] | add | [ǽnəməl] | animal |
| | [mæn] | man | [vəkǽbyulɛrɪ] | vocabulary |
| [a] | [nat] | not | [want] | want |
| | [ar] | are | [arǰəntínə] | Argentina |
| [ɔ] | [dɔg] | dog | [čóklət] | chocolate |
| | [nɔrɵ] | north | [ɔl] | all |
| [o] | [no] | know | [ónli] | only |
| | [go] | go | [mέksɪko] | Mexico |
| [ʊ] | [fʊl] | full | [plúrəl] | plural |
| | [fʊt] | foot | [bʊk] | book |
| [u] | [sun] | soon | [stúdənt] | student |
| | [ɾul] | rule | [yunɪvérsɪti] | university |
| [ə] | [kəm] | come | [əbə́v] | above |
| | [səm] | some | [əndərstǽnd] | understand |

| [aɪ] | [aɪ] | I | [ə́ndərlaɪn] | underline |
| | [paɪp] | pipe | [bɪsáɪd] | beside |
| [au] | [naun] | noun | [prónaun] | pronoun |
| | [saund] | sound | [taun] | town |
| [ɔɪ] | [bɔɪ] | boy | [ɔɪl] | oil |
| | [vɔɪs] | voice | [bɔɪl] | boil |

### Phrases

Pronounce the following groups of words. Pronounce each group of words as a unit. [1]
Do not separate the words in a group. Pronounce each group several times.

(a) [ðə lɛ́sən]  
    [ðə klæs]  
    [ðə daktər]  
    [ðə græmər klæs]

(b) [ɪz ɪmpɔ́rtənt]  
    [ɪz ízi]  
    [ɪz ɪ́ntrɪstɪŋ]  
    [ɪz byútɪful]

(c) [ðe əndərstǽnd]  
    [hi əndərstǽndz]  
    [wi ɛksplén]  
    [wi lə́rn]

---

[1] Note to the teacher: It is important that from the beginning students should group words into phrases and should pronounce the phrases as single words in order to counteract the Spanish tendency to give each word a separate stress, and even, especially in slow reading, a separate rising glide. The teacher may first find it necessary to pronounce the words separately so that the students may master the individual sounds. Then the teacher should pronounce the whole phrase rapidly with a single stress and with no separation of syllables. The pitch should be high on stressed syllables and low on unstressed syllables, and the students should be encouraged to mimic that pronunciation.

## LESSON II

### PRONUNCIATION

1. Hearing consonant contrasts
2. Voiced and voiceless sounds
3. Pronunciation of plurals of class 1 words and -s forms
   of class 2 words, phonetically determined

Review

a) Pronounce the key words in the Special Alphabet.

b) Identify the vowel sounds in the following words as the teacher pronounces them. (Use
   vowel chart from Lesson I.)

| | | | |
|---|---|---|---|
| [mæn] | [mɪt] | [met] | [lɛt] |
| [sun] | [lək] | [kat] | [pʊt] |
| [bot] | [bɔt] | [kot] | [kət] |

c) Pronounce the following groups of words with particular attention to the, a, an.

[ðə lɔŋ nəmbər]          [ə lɔŋ nəmbər]

[ðə nu bʊk]              [ə nu bʊk]

[ðə gʊd klæs]            [ə gʊd klæs]

[ðə dɪfɪkəlt wərd]       [ə dɪfɪkəlt wərd]

[ðə nu sɪmbəl]           [ə nu sɪmbəl]

[ən ælfəbɛt]             [ðɪ ælfəbɛt]

[ən ɛgzæmpəl]            [ðɪ ɛgzæmpəl]

[ən ɛksplənešən]         [ðɪ ɛksplənešən]

[ən izi ælfəbɛt]         [ðɪ izi ælfəbɛt]

[ən ɪntrɪstɪŋ ɛgzæmpəl]  [ðɪ ɪntrɪstɪŋ ɛgzæmpəl]

d) Pronounce the following sentences. Use the reduced forms.

[hu ɪz i]                [hwɛr ɪz i]

[hi laɪks ɪt]            [yu stədi]

[ɪz i ə studənt]         [ɪz ši bɪzi]

[ar wi let]              [wi notɪs ɪt]

23

## 1. Hearing consonant contrasts

Listen to the pronunciation of the following contrast.

        1.   [paɪ]

        2.   [baɪ]

The teacher will pronounce one of these syllables. Identify it by number. Identify the following contrasts in the same way.

| 1. | [taɪ] | [kaɪ] | [maɪ] | [faɪ] | [saɪ] | [haɪ] |
|---|---|---|---|---|---|---|
| 2. | [daɪ] | [gaɪ] | [naɪ] | [vaɪ] | [šaɪ] | [waɪ] |

| 1. | [baɪ] | [saɪ] | [daɪ] | [zaɪ] | [saɪ] | [šaɪ] |
|---|---|---|---|---|---|---|
| 2. | [vaɪ] | [Θaɪ] | [ðaɪ] | [ðaɪ] | [zaɪ] | [čaɪ] |

| 1. | [žaɪ] | [zaɪ] | [yaɪ] | [yaɪ] | [hwaɪ] | [am] |
|---|---|---|---|---|---|---|
| 2. | [ǰaɪ] | [žaɪ] | [zaɪ] | [ǰaɪ] | [waɪ] | [aŋ] |

        1.   [an]      [an]

        2.   [am]     [aŋ]

## 2. Voiced and voiceless sounds

Put your hands over your ears and pronounce [d]. Do you hear a buzzing sound? The sound which you hear is caused by the vibration of the vocal cords. Now pronounce [t] with your hands over your ears. Do you hear anything? No, because the vocal cords are not vibrating. There are only a few sounds in English which are pronounced without the voice.

$$[ \, p \ t \ k \ f \ \Theta \ s \ š \ č \ h \, ]$$

These are voiceless sounds.

All other sounds, including the vowel sounds, are pronounced with the vibration of the vocal cords. These are voiced sounds.

Notice that the only difference between the following sounds is the vibration of the vocal cords:

|  | | | | | Sibilants | | | |
|---|---|---|---|---|---|---|---|---|
| voiceless | [p | t | k | f | Θ | s | š | č | h] |
| voiced | [b | d | g | v | ð | z | ž | ǰ |

Pronounce the following sounds. Observe when they are voiced and when they are voice-less.

[ffff vvvv ffff vvvv]    [fvfvfv]

[ssss zzzz ssss zzzz]    [szszsz]

[šššš žžžž šš šš žžžž]    [šžšžšž]

Use the following chart of voiced and voiceless sounds for reference.

### VOICED SOUNDS

| Vowels: | [i] | | [u] | [aɪ] |
|---|---|---|---|---|
| | [ɪ] | | [ʊ] | [aʊ] |
| | [e] | | [o] | [ɔɪ] |
| | [ɛ] | [ə] | | |
| | [æ] | [a] | [ɔ] | |

| Consonants: | [b] | [m] | [v] | [l] |
|---|---|---|---|---|
| | [d] | [n] | [ð] | [r] |
| | [g] | [ŋ] | [z] | [w] |
| | [ǰ] | | [ž] | [y] |

### VOICELESS SOUNDS

| Consonants: | [p] | [f] | [h] |
|---|---|---|---|
| | [t] | [ɵ] | |
| | [k] | [s] | |
| | [č] | [š] | |

3. Pronunciation of plurals of class 1 words and -s forms of class 2 words, phonetically determined.

a) Class 1 words:

Pronounce the word class [klæs]. Pronounce the plural form: classes [klæsɪz].

Pronounce the plural of the following words by adding the separate syllable [ɪz].

| | | |
|---|---|---|
| [nərs] | [sɛ́ntəns] | [kɔrs] |
| [klæs] | [kǽmpəs] | [glæs] |
| [lənč] | [praɪs] | [pis] |

Notice that the plural ending is pronounced [ɪz] after a sibilant sound.

Pronounce the word <u>book</u> [bʊk]. Is the final sound voiced or voiceless?[1] It is voiceless, therefore we add the voiceless sound [s] to form the plural <u>books</u> [bʊks], but we do not pronounce an extra syllable.

Pronounce the word <u>dog</u> [dɔg]. Is the final sound voiced or voiceless? It is voiced, therefore we add the voiced sound [z][2] to form the plural <u>dogs</u> [dɔgz], but we do not pronounce an extra syllable.

Pronounce the plural form of the following words[3], and tell whether you are adding [s] or [z]. Example: <u>sounds</u> [saʊndz], <u>fruits</u> [fruts].

| | | | |
|---|---|---|---|
| [ǽlfəbɛt] | [tíčər] | [bɔɪ] | [dɪzɛ́rt] |
| [símbəl] | [ɪnstrə́ktər] | [stúdənt] | [frut] |
| [saʊnd] | [sup] | [dɛ́ntɪst] | [wərd] |
| [dáktər] | [mit] | [spun] | [kəp] |

b) Class 2 words:

The -s form of class 2 words (he <u>uses</u>) is pronounced in the same way as the plural forms of class 1 words. Pronounce the following words and add the separate syllable [ɪz] to produce the -s form. Example: <u>uses</u> [yuzɪz].

| | | |
|---|---|---|
| [ɛkskyuz] | [kɔz] | [yuz] |
| [ɛksprɛ́s] | [dɪskə́s] | [čenǰ] |
| [pæs] | [ɪnkrís] | [prənaʊ́ns] |

---

[1] It is the final <u>sound</u> which is significant, not the final letter. (e.g. in <u>envelope</u> the final letter is <u>e</u> but the final sound is [p].)

[2] This [z] is not pronounced with a strong buzzing sound. If the vowel is pronounced with the proper length, a weak or soft [s] may replace the [z].

[3] Notice that in all these words the plural form is spelled with <u>s</u>, but the pronunciation is often [z].

Pronounce the -s form of the following words, adding [s] or [z]. Do not pronounce an extra syllable. Example: <u>talks</u> [tɔks].

| | | |
|---|---|---|
| [omɪt] | [əraɪv] | [əndərstænd] |
| [rid] | [Ɵæŋk] | [go] |
| [ikwəl] | [it] | [drɪŋk] |
| [tek] | [tɔk] | [rɪpit] |
| [stədi] | [nid] | [æd] |

c) Exercises:

1. Form plurals of the following words:

| | | |
|---|---|---|
| book | lunch | fork |
| spoon | student | pen |
| fruit | word | class |
| glass | sentence | sound |

2. Use the correct form of the above words in the following sentences:

These are _____ .

The _____ are here.

3. Produce the -s form of the following words:

| | | | |
|---|---|---|---|
| [tek] | [rɪpít] | [pæs] | [prənauns] |
| [čenǰ] | [yuz] | [drɪŋk] | [it] |
| [dɪskəs] | [əndərstænd] | [stédi] | [nid] |

Use the correct form of the above words in the following sentence:

He usually _____ it.

Pronounce the following sentences:[1]

| | |
|---|---|
| [hi stədiz ⌐ɪŋglɪš] | [ši stədiz ⌐ɪŋglɪš] |
| [hi stédiz frɛnč] | [ši stédiz frɛnč] |
| [hi stédiz spǽnɪš] | [ši stédiz spǽnɪš] |
| [hi stədiz rəšən] | [ši stédiz réšən] |
| [hi stédiz ǰərmən] | [ši stédiz ǰərmən] |

---

[1]Note to the teacher: In these groups of sentences only the first sentence is marked with intonation. The other sentences in the group should be pronounced with similar intonation on the word in the same position.

[hi ‾stədiz ɪŋglɪš]
[hi raɪts íŋglɪš]
[hi spiks íŋglɪš]
[hi ridz íŋglɪš]
[hi əndərstǽndz ɪŋglɪš]

[ðə ‾bɔɪ‾ stədiz ɪŋglɪš]
[ðə gərl stədiz ɪŋglɪš]
[ðə daktər stədiz ɪŋglɪš]
[ðə nərs stədiz ɪŋglɪš]
[ðə ɛnǰɪnɪr stədiz ɪŋglɪš]

[ðə ‾bʊks‾ ər izi]
[ðə símbəlz ər ízi]
[ðə saʊndz ər ízi]
[ðə wərdz ər ízi]
[ðə lɛ́sənz ər ízi]

[ðe əndərstǽnd ðə ‾bʊks‾]
[ðe əndərstǽnd ðə símbəlz]
[ðe əndərstǽnd ðə saʊndz]
[ðe əndərstǽnd ðə wərdz]
[ðe əndərstǽnd ðə lɛ́sənz]

[ðə ‾plets‾ ər an ðə tébəl]
[ðə spunz ər an ðə tébəl]
[ðə fɔrks ər an ðə tébəl]
[ðə naɪvz ər an ðə tébəl]
[ðə kəps ər an ðə tébəl]
[ðə díšɪz ər an ðə tébəl]
[ðə glǽsɪz ər an ðə tébəl]

[ši ‾stədiz ɪŋglɪš]
[ši raɪts íŋglɪš]
[ši spiks íŋglɪš]
[ši ridz íŋglɪš]
[ši əndərstǽndz íŋglɪš]

[ðə ‾bɔɪ‾ ridz ‾ɪŋglɪš]
[ðə bɔɪ yúzɪz íŋglɪš]
[ðə bɔɪ dɪskə́sɪz íŋglɪš]
[ðə bɔɪ prənaʊ́nsɪz íŋglɪš]
[ðə bɔɪ spiks íŋglɪš]

[ðə bʊks ər ‾dɪ́fɪkəlt]
[ðə bʊks ər íntrɪstɪŋ]
[ðə bʊks ər ízi]
[ðə bʊks ər lɔŋ]
[ðə bʊks re šɔrt]

[ðə ‾stuḋənts əndərstǽnd ðə bʊks]
[ðə tíčərz əndərstǽnd ðə bʊks]
[ðə dáktərz əndərstǽnd ðə bʊks]
[ðə nə́rsɪz əndərstǽnd ðə bʊks]
[ðə bɔɪz əndərstǽnd ðə bʊks]

# LESSON III

## PRONUNCIATION

1. The organs of speech
2. Modification of sounds
3. Vowel production in general
4. Pronunciation of [i] and [ɪ]
5. Pronunciation of [t] and [d]
6. Pronunciation of -ed forms of verbs, phonetically determined


Review

a) Which of the following sounds are voiceless?

[ m b t i s ʃ l o f z ]

b) Pronounce the following sentences. Pay particular attention to the [s], [z] and [ɪz] endings.

1. [ðə studənts ər hɪr]

2. [ðə klæsɪz ər ɪntrɪstɪŋ]

3. [ðə saundz ər iżi]

4. [ðə daktərz yužuəli wɔrk]

5. [ðə bɔɪz stədi ɪŋglɪš]

6. [ši ɔlwɪz dɪskəsɪz ðə lɛsən]

7. [hi əndərstændz ðə klæs]

8. [ðə bɔɪ ɔlwɪz drɪŋks mɪlk]

9. [ši prənaunsɪz ðə wɔrdz]

10. [hi nidz ðə buks]

c) Use the correct form of the word in parenthesis in the following sentences. Example: The (book) are easy. The book are easy.

1. The (lunch) are good.
2. The teacher (like) the students.
3. The (student) understand the classes.
4. The student (repeat) the words.
5. The (fork) and (spoon) are on the table.
6. The new (symbol) are difficult.
7. The (pen) are on the desk.
8. Where are the (pencil)?
9. He (discuss) the lesson every day.
10. She (pronounce) the words.

## 1. The organs of speech

The parts of the body that are used in order to produce the sounds of speech are the organs of speech. Study the chart below.

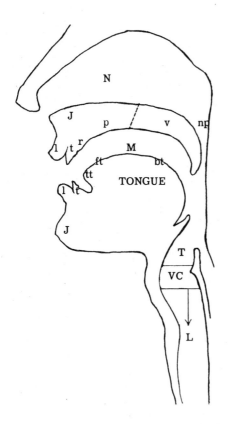

N  -  Nose
J  -  Jaw
M  -  Mouth
T  -  Throat
L  -  Lungs
VC -  Vocal cords

l  -  lips
t  -  teeth
r  -  tooth ridge
p  -  hard palate
v  -  velum

tt -  tip of tongue
ft -  front of tongue
mt -  middle of tongue
bt -  back of tongue
np -  nasal passage

DIAGRAM OF THE ORGANS OF SPEECH

The Vocal Cords

The vocal cords are in the throat. They are two muscular ledges that are similar to the lips. They may open and close. During breathing and during the production of voiceless sounds, the vocal cords are apart, or open.[1] Pronounce the following voiceless sounds: [ s, Θ, t, p, č, k, f, š, h ]. The vocal cords are not vibrating.

During voicing they open and close very rapidly. Pronounce the following voiced sounds [ z, ð, d, b, ǰ, g, v, ž, i, e, a, u ]. The vocal cords are vibrating.

During a whisper the back part of the vocal cords is open, but the front part is frequently closed. Do not whisper when practicing pronunciation since it is difficult to distinguish voiced and voiceless sounds.

### Description of the Organs of Speech

(This description is to be used for reference.)

The sounds of English are all produced by air which comes from the lungs into the throat and then passes through the mouth or the nose. Contraction of the lungs expels the air. The other organs of speech modify this stream of air in order to produce sounds. The organs of speech are as follows:

A. Movable speech organs

Lungs (L in the diagram)

    Contraction of the lungs expels the air.

Vocal cords (VC in the diagram)

    In the throat (T in the diagram) the air passes through the opening between the vocal cords. When the air, going through this opening, causes the vocal cords to vibrate, a "voiced" sound is produced. When the vocal cords do not vibrate, a "voiceless" sound is produced.

Lower jaw

    The lower jaw can move down increasing the size of the mouth cavity (M in the diagram).

Tongue (Tongue in the diagram)

    The tongue can move in many ways.

    a) The tip of the tongue (tt in the diagram) may go between the teeth as in the sound [Θ]. It may turn up and back in the mouth as in several [r] sounds.

    b) The front of the tongue (ft in the diagram) is the flat part of the tongue just behind the tip. The front of the tongue may move up or down, or it may form a small groove as in the sound [š].

    c) The middle of the tongue (mt in the diagram) may be raised as in [i], or it can touch the top of the mouth as in [k].

    d) The movement of the back of the tongue (bt in the diagram) is similar to the movement of the middle of the tongue.

---

[1]Review the difference in pronunciation of voiceless and voiced sounds in Lesson II, Pronunciation.

Lips (l in the diagram)

The lips may close as in the sound [p], or they may form an opening as in the sound [u].

Velum (v in the diagram)

The velum can be lowered so that the air goes through the nose (N in the diagram) as in [m]; or it may be raised in order to close the nasal passage (np in the diagram) as in [a].

B. Immovable speech organs

Teeth (t in the diagram)

The teeth affect the air when it leaves the mouth, and they often affect the position of the tip of the tongue or the lower jaw.

Tooth ridge (r in the diagram)

The tooth ridge is the upper gum. The tooth ridge is touched by the tip of the tongue in pronouncing [t], [d], [n].

Palate (p in the diagram)

The hard palate is the upper front part of the mouth. It helps in the production of many sounds in English.

2. Modification of sounds, especially related to vowel sounds

a) The lips may be rounded so that they have a circular opening between them. The opening is large when they are only slightly rounded. Pronounce [ɔ]. The opening is small when they are very much rounded. Pronounce [u]. The lips may be unrounded so that they are parallel to each other and the opening between them is flat. Pronounce [e].

Use a mirror in the following exercise. Round and unround the lips. Produce the sound [a] with the lips rounded. Continue the sound [a] and unround the lips; do not change the position of the tongue. Observe the change in sound.

Use a mirror in the following exercise. Pronounce the vowel sounds [ i, e, o, ɔ, u ]. Which vowels are produced with the lips rounded? Which vowels are produced with the lips unrounded?

Pronounce the vowel [i]. Continue the sound [i] and round the lips; do not change the position of the tongue. Pronounce the vowel [u]. Continue the sound [u] and unround the lips; do not change the position of the tongue.

b) The tongue may be somewhat front in the mouth, [i], or it may be farther back in the mouth, [u]. Pronounce the following sounds. Determine which sounds are produced with the tongue farther back in the mouth:

[i] or [u]    [o] or [e]    [a] or [ɔ]

c) The muscles of the tongue and throat may be tense or relaxed. Pronounce [i] with the muscles relatively tense. Pronounce [ɪ]. The muscles are more relaxed. Determine which of the following sounds are pronounced with more tenseness of the muscles:

[e] or [ɛ]    [æ] or [a]    [u] or [ʊ]

## 3. Vowel Production in general[1]

Pronounce [kɔfi kɔfi kɔfi kɔfi]. Notice that the two vowels in the word are the most prominent and loudest part of the word and that the word has two syllables.

Whenever a vowel occurs in a word there is a syllable. Vowels are more resonant in syllables than consonants; they are syllabic sounds. In the production of vowel sounds there is no interruption of the air stream in the mouth. Pronounce [ a, i, o ]. Air is expelled from the lungs by the chest or the abdominal muscles. The air passes through the mouth. The sound that you hear is the vibration of the vocal cords. Vowels are voiced sounds in normal speech.

A diagram conveniently indicates the position of the tongue during the pronunciation of vowels. The diagram usually has three vertical sections and three horizontal sections. Notice the position of the vowels in the following diagram.

|  |  | Front | Central | Back |
|---|---|---|---|---|
| High | T | [i] |  | [u] |
|  | R | [ɪ] |  | [ʊ] |
| Mid | T | [e] |  | [o] |
|  | R | [ɛ] | [ə] |  |
| Low | T | [æ] |  | [ɔ] |
|  | R |  | [a] |  |

T    Tense muscles of throat and tongue

R    Relaxed muscles of throat and tongue

[1] The following is a comparison of the relative position of English vowels and Spanish vowels. This chart can be referred to as the individual vowels are presented. Spanish vowels are represented by the large dark letters.

|  | Front | Central | Back |
|---|---|---|---|
| High | [i] O  [ɪ] | | [u]  [ʊ] |
| Mid | [e]  [ɛ] | [ə] | [o] |
| Low | [æ] | [a] | [ɔ] |

The following diagrams indicate some of the positions of the tongue.

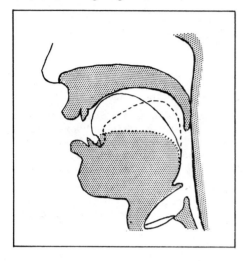

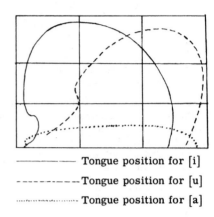

——————— Tongue position for [i]

--------- Tongue position for [u]

················· Tongue position for [a]

Notice the pronunciation of the vowels in the following words. They are usually pronounced very long.

| | | |
|---|---|---|
| leave [i] | man [æ] | coat [o] |
| sit   [ɪ] | not  [a] | foot  [ʊ] |
| make [e] | but  [ə] | soon [u] |
| bed   [ɛ] | wall [ɔ] | |

## 4. Pronunciation of [i] and [ɪ]

In the vowel [i] the position of the tongue is <u>high front</u>; the lips are <u>unrounded</u> and the muscles are tense.

In the vowel [ɪ] the position of the tongue is not as high as in [i]; the lips are <u>unrounded</u> and the muscles are more relaxed than in [i].

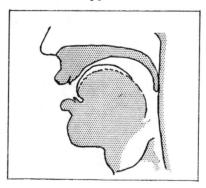

Pronounce the following words:

|  1 [i] | 2 [ɪ] |
|--------|-------|
| [lid]  | [lɪd] |
| [did]  | [dɪd] |
| [liv]  | [lɪv] |
| [kin]  | [kɪn] |
| [čip]  | [čɪp] |
| [fil]  | [fɪl] |
| [pik]  | [pɪk] |
| [dil]  | [dɪl] |
| [fit]  | [fɪt] |

Pronounce the following pairs of sentences:

(a)  1. The man beat [bit] the dog.
     2. The man bit   [bɪt] the dog.

(b)  1. He's going to leave [liv].
     2. He's going to live   [lɪv].

(c)  1. This is a sheep [šip].
     2. This is a ship   [šɪp].

Pronounce the following groups of words:

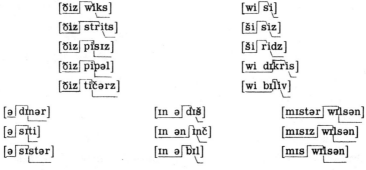

[ðiz wɪks]                   [wi si]

[ðiz strits]                 [ši siz]

[ðiz pisɪz]                 [ši ridz]

[ðiz pipəl]                [wi dɪkris]

[ðiz tičərz]               [wi bɪliv]

[ə dɪnər]        [ɪn ə dɪš]       [mɪstər wɪlsən]

[ə siti]          [ɪn ən ɪnč]     [mɪsɪz wɪlsən]

[ə sɪstər]       [ɪn ə bɪl]       [mɪs wɪlsən]

Memorize the following conversation:

Student A.  [mɪstər wɪlsən ɪz ə tičər]

Student B.  [hi tičɪz prənənsiešən]

Student A.  [yɛs æn hɪz vɛri ɪntrɪstɪŋ]

## 5. Pronunciation of [t] and [d][1]

The tongue touches the tooth ridge in the pronunciation of [t] and [d]. <u>The tongue does not touch the teeth</u>. The sound [t] is a voiceless sound and [d] is voiced.

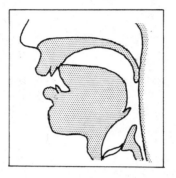

Tongue position for [t] and [d]

A paper held in front of the mouth will vibrate when you pronounce [t] but not when you pronounce [d]. Observe this in the pronunciation of the following:

[t - t - t - t - t - t]                    [d - d - d - d - d - d]

[ti]  [taɪ]  [to]  [tu]  [tɔɪ]            [di]  [daɪ]  [de]  [do]  [du]

[it]  [et]  [æt]  [ot]  [aʊt]             [od]  [aɪd]  [ed]  [æd]  [ɛd]

[tam  ɪz  æz  tɔl  æz  tɪm]

[dæn  ɪz  æz  dark  æz  dɛv]

## 6. Pronunciation of -ed forms of verbs, phonetically determined

Pronounce the following pairs of words:

|                        |                           |
|------------------------|---------------------------|
| repeat [rɪpít]         | repeated [rɪpítɪd]        |
| add [æd]               | added [ǽdɪd]              |

Notice that we add the separate syllable [ɪd] when the simple form of the word ends in the sounds [t] or [d].

Pronounce the -ed from of the following words:

| [nid]   | [æksɛ́pt]  | [índɪket]  |
|---------|-----------|------------|
| [æd]    | [omít]    | [səksíd]   |
| [ɛnd]   | [prɪsíd]  | [want]     |

---

[1] Note to the teacher: These two sounds are introduced here to prepare the student to use them in pronouncing the -ed forms of verbs. A more complete explanation with diagram and exercises will be found in Lesson XII.

Pronounce the following pair of words:

live [lɪv]           lived [lɪvd]

Notice that we add [d] because the final sound in [lɪvd] is voiced.[1] Do not add an extra syllable.

Pronounce the following pair of words:

miss [mɪs]           missed [mɪst]

Notice that we add [t] because the final sound of [mɪs] is voiceless. Do not add an extra syllable.

Pronounce the -ed form of the following words:

| | | | |
|---|---|---|---|
| [yuz] | [tɔk] | [swálo] | [dɪskə́s] |
| [kɔz] | [laɪk] | [stə́di] | [prənaúns] |
| [mɪs] | [pæs] | [íkwəl] | [ɛksprés] |
| [lɪv] | [sərv] | [ǽnsər] | [ɛkskyúz] |

Pronounce the -ed form of the following words. Add a separate syllable in the pronunciation only when the final sound is [t] or [d].

| | | |
|---|---|---|
| like | indicate | discuss |
| taste | pass | study |
| serve | excuse | accept |
| miss | need | express |
| add | omit | pronounce |

Use the -ed form of the words from the above list in the following sentences:

I _____ it yesterday.

I _____ them yesterday.

Pronounce the following sentences:

| | |
|---|---|
| [ðə bɔɪ laɪkt ɪŋglɪš] | [ši laɪkt ɪŋglɪš] |
| [ðə bɔɪ laɪkt spǽnɪš] | [ši laɪkt spǽnɪš] |
| [ðə bɔɪ laɪkt frɛnč] | [ši laɪkt frɛnč] |
| [ðə bɔɪ nídɪd ɪŋglɪš] | [ši nídɪd ɪŋglɪš] |
| [ðə bɔɪ nídɪd spǽnɪš] | [ši nídɪd spǽnɪš] |
| [ðə bɔɪ nídɪd frɛnč] | [ši nídɪd frɛnč] |

---

[1] Do not over-emphasize the pronunciation of [d]. It is helpful to lengthen the vowel sound preceding the [d] rather than make the [d] too strong.

[hi ⌐laɪkt⌐ ɪŋglɪš]                    [ðe ⌐laɪkt⌐ ɪŋglɪš]

[hi nídɪd íŋglɪš]                      [ðe nídɪd íŋglɪš]

[hi prənaúnst íŋglɪš]                  [ðe prənaúnst íŋglɪš]

[hi dɪskə́st íŋglɪš]                   [ðe dɪskə́st íŋglɪš]

[hi stə́did íŋglɪš]                    [ðe stə́did íŋglɪš]

## LESSON IV

### PRONUNCIATION

1. Pronunciation of [e] and [ɛ]
2. Pronunciation of [ɛ] and [ɪ]
3. Pronunciation of [r] (after vowels)
4. Intonation
5. 2-4 intonation curve
6. Intonation of the pattern ENGLISH CLASS, TEA CUP, etc.

Review

a) Review the following conversation from memory:

Student A. Mr. Wilson is a teacher.
Student B. He teaches pronunciation.
Student A. Yes, and he's very interesting.

b) Pronounce the following pair of sentences:

This is a sheep.                              This is a ship.

c) Pronounce the following sentences. Pay particular attention to the [t], [d], and [ɪd] endings.

1. [aɪ stədid ðə lɛsən]
2. [ši ɛksplend ðə prɑbləm]
3. [hi rɪpitɪd ðə wɚdz]
4. [ðe prənaunst ðə wɚdz]
5. [ðə lɛtər əraɪvd yɛstərdi]
6. [ðe lɪvd ɪn pərᵾ]
7. [hi wantɪd ə nu bᵾk]
8. [ðə tičər ænsərd ðə kwɛsčənz]
9. [ðe nidɪd ə pɛn]
10. [ðə studənts ətɛndɪd ðə klæs]

d) Use the past form of the word in parenthesis in the following sentences:

Example: They (answer) the question.  They answered the question.

1. They (use) a new book.
2. The teacher (discuss) the lesson.
3. We (pronounce) many words.
4. The doctor (work) at night.
5. The boys (study) in their rooms.
6. They (like) all of the people.
7. The students (arrive) at 10 o'clock.
8. She (live) in Colombia.
9. The teacher (answer) a question.
10. They (like) the food.

39

1. Pronunciation of [e] and [ɛ]

During the pronunciation of the vowel [e] the tongue position changes. The tongue begins in a <u>mid front tense</u> position. Then the tongue rises toward a high front position. This change in position causes the vowel to be slightly diphthongized.[1]

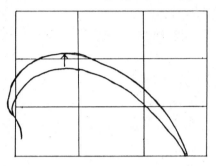

The change in tongue position for [e]

In the vowel [ɛ] the tongue position is <u>mid front</u> in a lower position than for [e] and the muscles are <u>lax</u>.

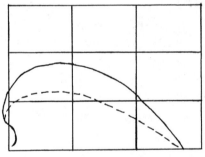

————— Tongue position of [e] non-diphthongized

- - - - - -Tongue position of [ɛ]

---

[1] Note to the teacher: If one wishes to symbolize the diphthongization he can indicate the sound by the symbol [eɪ]. This can be used during the first period in teaching this sound because it helps to remind the student of the gliding quality in this vowel.

Pronounce the following words:

| 1 [e] | 2 [ɛ] |
|-------|-------|
| [pen] | [pɛn] |
| [sel] | [sɛl] |
| [met] | [mɛt] |
| [bet] | [bɛt] |
| [led] | [lɛd] |
| [wet] | [wɛt] |
| [let] | [lɛt] |

Pronounce the following pairs of sentences:

(a)  1. He has a pain [pen].
     2. He has a pen  [pɛn].

(b)  1. They are going to sail [sel] the boat.
     2. They are going to sell [sɛl] the boat.

Pronounce the following groups of words:

| | |
|---|---|
| [ɪts ə ˈlɛtər] | [ɪts ə ˈnem] |
| [sɛnd ə ˈlɛtər] | [ətɛnd ə ˈklæs] |
| [mek ə ˈdɛt] | [ðə sem ˈplet] |
| [hiz ə ˈfrɛnd] | [ðə sem ˈlɛtər] |
| [hiz ə ˈgɛst] | [nɛvər ˈlet] |
| [si ðə ˈledi] | [gɛt ə ˈlɛtər] |
| [ðə sem ˈledi] | [spɛnd ðə ˈməni] |

Memorize the following conversation:

Student A.  [du wi hæv ən ɛgzæmɪneʃən təde]

Student B.  [yɛs ɪts goɪŋ tə bi æt tɛn]

2. Pronunciation of [ɛ] and [ɪ][1]

Notice the difference in tongue position for the sounds [ɛ] and [ɪ].

---

[1] Note to the teacher: The distinction between [ɛ] and [ɪ] is likely to be more difficult than the distinction between [e] and [ɛ] and needs special attention.

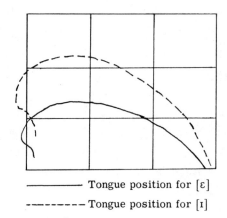

——————— Tongue position for [ɛ]

- - - - - - - Tongue position for [ɪ]

Pronounce the following words:[1]

| 1 [ɪ] | 2 [ɛ] |
|---|---|
| [pɪn] | [pɛn] |
| [sɪl] | [sɛl] |
| [mɪt] | [mɛt] |
| [bɪt] | [bɛt] |
| [lɪd] | [lɛd] |
| [wɪt] | [wɛt] |
| [lɪt] | [lɛt] |

Pronounce the following pairs of sentences:

(a)  1. She has a red pin [pɪn].
     2. She has a red pen [pɛn].

(b)  1. This is bitter [bɪtər] tea.
     2. This is better [bɛtər] tea.

Memorize the following conversation:

Teacher A. [hwɛn du wi it dɪnər]

Teacher B. [æt sɪks əklàk]

Teacher A. [ɪts sɪks tɛn aɪm lèt]

3. Pronunciation of [r] after vowels

An English [r] can be produced with the tongue in several different positions. English speakers, however, usually produce the following kind of [r].

---

[1]Note to the teacher: The sounds [ɪ] and [ɛ] can also be contrasted with [i] if this seems advisable.

At the beginning of the [r] sound the tip of the tongue is turned up sharply toward the palate and the lips are slightly rounded. The voiced sound is continuous from the vowel sound to the [r] sound which follows it.

Notice that there is no  contact  of the tongue with the palate and the tongue does not vibrate.

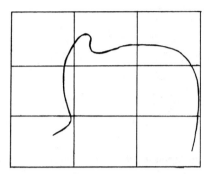

Tongue position for [r]

Pronounce [a]; then during the sound, turn the tip of the tongue up toward the palate. Perform the same experiment and tighten the muscles of the throat.

Pronounce the following words and sentences:

| | | | | |
|---|---|---|---|---|
| [ɔ̇r] | [ȧr] | [ɛ̇r] | [ïr] | [u̇r] |
| [pɔ̇r] | [k̇ar] | [fɛ̇r] | [ḣɪr] | [pu̇r] |
| [mȧr] | [fȧr] | [hwɛ̇r] | [nɪ̇r] | [pyu̇r] |
| [stɔ̇r] | [stȧr] | [ðɛ̇r] | [wɪ̇r] | [kyu̇r] |
| [kwɔrtər] | [gardən] | [kɛṙful] | [nɪṙli] | [šu̇rli] |

[hwɛr ər ðə ḇuks]

[ðə buks ər hɪr]

[ðə stɔr ɪz far frəm hɪr]

[ðə kar ɪz nɪr ðə haus]

Memorize the following conversation:

Doctor A. [hwɛr ər yə goɪŋ]

Doctor B. [aɪm goɪŋ tə ðə stɔr]

Doctor A. [ɪz ɪt far frəm hɪr]

Doctor B. [no ɪts vɛri nɪr]

## 4. Intonation

Intonation changes the meaning of sentences in English. If you do not use the accepted intonation forms, people will not understand you.

English uses four pitches or tones. These four pitches are not absolute tones equivalent to precise musical notes. They are related to each other. For convenience we represent American English pitch as follows:

$$\overline{\text{la}} \text{ (extra high)} \qquad 1$$
$$\overline{\text{la}} \text{ (usual stressed tone)} \quad 2$$
$$\underline{\text{la}} \text{ (normal)} \qquad 3$$
$$\text{la (low, final)} \qquad 4$$

A <u>vertical</u> line indicates that the pitch changes between syllables.

lə ⌐ la ⌐ lə

A <u>diagonal</u> or sloping line indicates that the pitch changes within a syllable.

lə ⌐ la﹨

Read the following syllables and groups of words slowly. Then read them rapidly. Then make the interval between pitches very small and very great.[1]

---

[1] Note to the teacher: There are two varieties of pitch sequences, the formal type of basal sentence endings used in ordinary, calm statements of fact, such as the 2-4 pattern to be taught in this lesson, and the type expressive of various emotions. In these lessons attention is first given to the basal, formal types for student production and later to the expressive types for recognition.

In this exercise there is some practice in varied sequences in order to train students in hearing differences. Students who have difficulty may hear the pitches more readily if they are whistled, or hummed, or played on a slide whistle. In the first exercises very slow reading with separated syllables and exaggerated pitch changes may also help the students to notice the pitch changes. Once the students can hear the pitch changes, however, it is advisable to repeat the syllables rapidly, particularly in the sample sentences, since slow, exaggerated delivery sounds different from normal delivery.

Individual speakers of English vary considerably in the pitch intervals which they use, but the general pitch system of four levels remains very much the same. Pronounce pitch three with your ordinary basal tone; pitch two at your normal height for stressed syllables; pitch four at your normal utterance of unstressed syllables at the end of a statement.

Speech includes pitch, speed, and rhythmic grouping. The instructions to pronounce a phrase as a single word have been designed to assist rhythmic utterance. In this exercise stressed vowels are written [a] and unstressed vowels [ə] to the same end.

a)  də da də   ðə lɛsən          də da də   ðɪs mɔrnɪŋ
    də da də   ðə tičər          də da də   ðɪs ivnɪŋ

b)  də da də   spik sloli        də da də   ə daktər
    də da də   spik klɪrli       də da də   ə lɔyər

c)  da da      yɛs yɛs           da da      jan jan
    da da      no no             da da      jɪm jɪm

d)  də da      ðə klæs           də də da   tə ðə klæs
    də da      ðə pɛn            də də dá   tə ðə rúm

e)  [ɪn ðə haʊs]                 [ɪn ðə haʊs]
    [an ðə dɛsk]                 [an ðə dɛsk]
    [frəm ðə yunɪvərsɪti]        [frəm ðə yunɪvərsɪti]

## 5. The 2-4 intonation curve

The sequence of pitches or the rise and fall of the voice in a sentence is the intonation of the sentence.  Listen to the following sentence.

The lesson is difficult.

The most significant part of the intonation of this sentence is the intonation curve of the word underline{difficult}. The most important intonation curve of a sentence begins at the last heavily stressed syllable of the sentence.

Pronounce the following phrase.

in the city

The word that is emphasized in this group of words is city. The accented syllable is pronounced on pitch 2. The syllable that follows is pronounced on pitch 4. This is called 2-4 intonation. We can emphasize the important part of a sentence by using the 2-4 intonation.

Pronounce the following phrases with 2-4 intonation.

[æt hom]                          [ðə bʊk]
[ðə studənt]                      [ə daktər]
[ɪz rɪdɪŋ]                        [ɪz ɪntrɪstɪŋ]
[ðə yunɪvərsɪti]                  [ðə klæs]

Pronounce the following sentence in imitation of the teacher.

[ðə studənts kloz ðɛr bʊks]

The last word that is emphasized in this sentence is [bʊks]. Notice the change of pitch on this word. In English the change of tone or pitch on the last emphasized word is most important

Pronounce the following sentences:

[ši əndərstændz ðə⌐kwɛščənz]

[ðə mɛn ər æt⌐hɑm]

[ðə mægəzinz ər vɛri⌐ɪntrɪstɪŋ]

[šiz ə byutɪful⌐wumən]

Which words are emphasized in the following sentences?

[hwɛr ɪz ðə⌐mæn]     [hwɛr ar yu⌐frəm]

Pronounce the following sentences:

[hwət ɪz ər⌐nɛm]

[hwɛn ɪz i⌐kəmɪŋ]

[ɪz i ə⌐tičər]

[dəz i laɪk⌐mɪlk]

Notice that we can use the same intonation in questions that we use in statements. Pronounce the following sentences as marked:

[hwət ɪz ɪz⌐nɛm]                    [hwɛn ɪz i⌐goɪŋ]

[hwət ɪz ɪz⌐kəntri]                 [hwɛn ɪz i⌐kəmɪŋ]

[ɪz i ə⌐tičər]                      [dəz i laɪk⌐mɪlk]

[ɪz i ə⌐studənt]                    [dəz i laɪk⌐wɔtər]

[ɪz i ə⌐daktər]                     [dəz i laɪk⌐kɔfi]

[ɪz i ə⌐lɔyər]                      [dəz i laɪk⌐frut]

Mark the following sentences with 2-4 intonation. Emphasize the last important word.

1. [ðə stúdənts kloz ðɛr buks]

2. [ši əndərstǽndz ðə kwésčənz]

3. [hwɛr ər ðə mɛn]

4. [ðe ər stə́dɪŋ æt ðə yunɪvə́rsɪti]

5. [ðə kófi ɪz swit]

6. [ðə mægəzínz ər íntrɪstɪŋ]

7. [ar ðə dáktərz góɪŋ tə go]

8. [ðə yəŋ gərlz wər rídɪŋ]

9. [šiz ə byútɪful wúmən]

10. [ðə mæn wɔkt tə klæs yéstərdi]

11. [ɪz ðə stúdənt ə dáktər]

12. [ðə mæn spiks ɪŋglɪš]

13. [dəz ši əténd ðə yunıvársıti]

14. [dıd ðə stúdənts rısív sévrəl létərs]

15. [ðı ínglıš lǽŋgwıǰ ız véri dífıkəlt]

## 6. Intonation of the pattern ENGLISH CLASS, TEA CUP, etc.

The teacher will pronounce the following phrases. Mimic his intonation.[1]

| (a) | (b) | (c) | (d) |
|-----|-----|-----|-----|
| English class | tea cup | post office | telephone book |
| grammar class | drug store | phone number | vocabulary class |
| Spanish class | shoe store | word order | English teacher |
| coffee cup | book store | pronunciation class | Spanish teacher |

Pronounce the following sentences. Pay particular attention to the intonation.

This is an English class.

This is a grammar class.

This is a Spanish class.

This is a pronunciation class.

This is a vocabulary class.

The English class is important.

The grammar class is important.

The Spanish class is important.

The pronunciation class is important.

The vocabulary class is important.

He's an English teacher.

He's a Spanish teacher.

He's a French teacher.

The English teacher is interesting.

The Spanish teacher is interesting.

The French teacher is interesting.

Where is the post office?

Where is the drug store?

Where is the shoe store?

Where is the book store?

The post office is on Main Street.

The drug store is on Main Street.

The shoe store is on Main Street.

The book store is on Main Street.

---

[1] Note to the teacher: The tendency of students is to emphasize the last word in these word groups. They need practice in using the 2-4 intonation on the first element of these groups.

# LESSON V

## PRONUNCIATION

1. Pronunciation of [æ]
2. Pronunciation of [r] before vowels
3. 2-3  2-4 intonation
4. Reduced form of GOING TO
5. Pronunciation of negative forms
6. Change of vowel in unaccented syllable

Review

a) Review these conversations from memory.

1.   Student A.  Do we have an examination today?
     Student B.  Yes, it's going to be at ten.

2.   Teacher A.  When do we eat dinner?
     Teacher B.  At six o'clock.
     Teacher A.  It's six ten. I'm late.

3.   Doctor A.   Where are you going?
     Doctor B.   I'm going to the store.
     Doctor A.   Is it far from here?
     Doctor B.   No. It's very near.

b) Pronounce the following sentences with the 2-4 intonation as marked.

The man is a doctor.            He's from Colombia.

He's studying English.         Is he a good student?

What country is he from?        Yes, he studies very much.

1. Pronunciation of [æ]

The sound [æ] is pronounced with tongue relaxed in low front position. The tip of the tongue touches the back of the lower teeth. The lips are spread as in a smile. The muscles of the throat are tense.

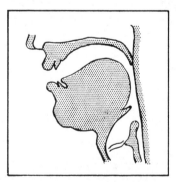

Tongue Position for [æ]

48

The sound [æ] is pronounced with the tongue in a <u>lower</u> position than for [ɛ]. Notice the difference in tongue position between the two sounds in the diagram below.

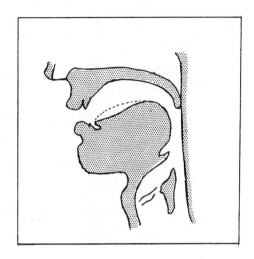

———————— Tongue position in [æ]

------------- Tongue position in [ɛ]

Pronounce the following words:

| 1 [æ] | 2 [ɛ] |
|-------|-------|
| [æd] | [ɛd] |
| [mæn] | [mɛn] |
| [sæd] | [sɛd] |
| [pæn] | [pɛn] |
| [læd] | [lɛd] |
| [læs] | [lɛs] |
| [bæd] | [bɛd] |
| [bæt] | [bɛt] |
| [sæl] | [sɛl] |

Pronounce the following pair of sentences:

The man [mæn] wanted a letter.

The men [mɛn] wanted a letter.

Pronounce the following:[1]

| | | |
|---|---|---|
| [æd] | [mæn] | [hæt] |
| [sæt] | [læst] | [æsk] |
| [fæst] | [pæn] | [æftərnun] |
| [bæd] | [læk] | [ðe it fæst] |
| [əndərstænd] | [glæs] | [ðe rən fæst] |
| [læŋgwɪ̌ǰ] | [blækbɔrd] | [ðe raɪt fæst] |
| [kæmpəs] | [stæmp] | [ðe wɔk fæst] |
| [kæš ə čɛk] | [an ðə kæmpəs] | |
| [æsk ə kwɛsčən] | [aɪ əndərstænd] | |
| [tu glæsɪz] | [ɪn ðə klæs] | |
| [ðɪs æftərnun] | [an ðə blækbɔrd] | |

[hwɛr ɪz yər hæt]      [ɪts an ðə ræk]

[ɪz yər hæt blæk]      [no ɪts tæn]

Memorize the following conversation:

Engineer A. [hwɛrz ðə mæn]

Engineer B. [hiz ɪn klæs]

## 2. Pronunciation of [r] before vowels

The [r] sound is pronounced by raising the tip of the tongue toward the top of the mouth. The tongue does not touch the top of the mouth. Pronounce car, store, near, more, there, far, here, where.

In pronouncing [r] at the beginning of words or syllables there is no contact or vibration of the tongue against the top of the mouth. Pronounce room [rum]. Lips are rounded. Pronounce read [rid] and look in a mirror. Practice pronouncing [r] very slowly with rounded lips.[2]

---

[1]All words in this list are spelled with a and pronounced [æ]: ask [æsk]; bad [bæd], etc. The teacher should point this out to the student as being one of the regularities of English spelling. He should caution the student, however, that the exceptions are many.

[2]Note to the teacher: For Spanish-speaking students and others who use a flap [r] in their own language use the following exercise: Pronounce Spanish flap [r]. Turn the tongue back until it can no longer touch the roof of the mouth. Round lips and continue to pronounce [r]. It will approximate the American [r]. (For a fuller description of this technique, see article by Robert Lado, Language Learning, Volume I, Number 3, pp. 20-23.)

Pronounce the following:

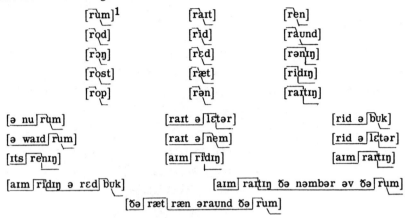

[ə nuꜰrʌm]          [raɪt əʃlɛtər]          [rid əʃbʊk]

[ə waɪdꜰrʌm]          [raɪt əʃnɛm]          [rid əʃlɛtər]

[ɪtsꜰrenɪŋ]          [aɪmꜰrɪdɪŋ]          [aɪmꜰraɪtɪŋ]

[aɪmꜰrɪdɪŋ ə rɛdꜰbʊk]          [aɪmꜰraɪtɪŋ ðə nəmbər əv ðəꜰrʌm]

[ðəꜰrætꜰræn əraund ðəꜰrum]

Memorize the following conversations:

Doctor A. [hwɛr ɪz yərꜰrʌm]

Doctor B. [ɪts nɪr ðəꜰrækəm bɪldɪŋ]

Lawyer A. [du yə ridꜰɪŋglɪš]

Lawyer B. [yɛs aɪꜰrid ænꜰraɪt ɪŋglɪš]

## 3. 2-3   2-4 intonation

Pronounce the following sentences after the teacher.

a)          [ðə prəfɛsər tičɪz ðəʃlɛsən]

In this sentence we are emphasizing lesson. We use the 2-4 intonation to emphasize.

b)          [ðə prəfɛsər tičɪz ðəʃlɛsən]

In this sentence we are emphasizing or pointing out professor and lesson. Notice that we are using the 2-4 intonation to emphasize these two words.

If we want to pronounce this sentence more rapidly, we say

c)          [ðə prəfɛsər tičɪz ðəʃlɛsən]

Notice the difference in intonation between sentence (b) and sentence (c). In sentence (b) the intonation on professor is 2-4 and in sentence (c) it is 2-3. When we want to pronounce longer sentences more rapidly and we want to emphasize more than one word, we use the 2-3 intonation in the middle of the sentence and 2-4 at the end.

---

[1]Note to the teacher: Practice the [r] sound before rounded vowels first so that the student will automatically round the lips. Then practice the [r] sound before unrounded vowels.

Pronounce the following sentences after the teacher:

a) [ðə ˈtiʧər hæz ə ˈbʊk]
[ðə ˈtiʧər hæz ə ˈlæmp]
[ðə ˈtiʧər hæz ə ˈpaɪp]
[ðə ˈtiʧər hæz ə ˈwaɪf]
[ðə ˈtiʧər hæz ə ˈbʊk]

b) [hi ˈstədiz ðə ˈlɛsən]
[ši ˈstədiz ðə ˈlɛsən]
[wi ˈstədi ðə ˈlɛsən]
[hi ˈænsərz ðə ˈkwɛsʧənz]
[ši ˈænsərz ðə ˈkwɛsʧənz]
[wi ˈænsər ðə ˈkwɛsʧənz]
[hi ˈnoʊtɪsɪz ðə ˈtiʧər]
[ši ˈnoʊtɪsɪz ðə ˈtiʧər]
[wi ˈnoʊtɪs ðə ˈtiʧər]

c) [maɪ ˈdɔtər wəz ˈbɪzi]
[hɪz ˈdɔtər wəz ˈbɪzi]
[hər ˈdɔtər wəz ˈbɪzi]
[hɪz ˈænsər wəz ˈšɔrt]
[hər ˈænsər wəz ˈšɔrt]
[ar ˈbrɛkfəst wəz ˈərli]
[ðɛr ˈdɪnər wəz ˈərli]
[hɪz ˈfaðər wəz ˈbɪzi]

d) [ðə ˈkɑfi wəz ɪkˈspɛnsɪv]
[ðə ˈtiʧər wəz ˈyəŋ]
[ðə ˈtiʧərz wər ˈyəŋ]
[ðə ˈbətər wəz ɪkˈspɛnsɪv]
[ðɪ ˈænsərz wər ˈpərfɪkt]
[ðə ˈwʊmən wəz ˈərli]
[ðə ˈlɛdi wəz ˈyəŋ]
[ðə ˈlɛdiz wər ˈyəŋ]

## 4. Reduced form of GOING TO

Notice the reduced form of <u>going to</u> in the following sentences.[1]

[hiz goıŋ tə⌐rɪd]                    [ðə bɔız ər goıŋ tə⌐rɪd]

[hiz goıŋ tə⌐raɪt]                   [ðə bɔız ər goıŋ tə⌐raɪt]

[hiz goıŋ tə⌐sıŋ]                    [ðə bɔız ər goıŋ tə⌐sıŋ]

[hiz goıŋ tə⌐tɔk]                    [ðə bɔız ər goıŋ tə⌐tɔk]

## 5. Pronunciation of negative forms

Practice the following sentences:

[hi ízənt ə⌐daktər]                  [ši də́zənt⌐rɪd]

[ši ízənt ə dáktər]                  [ši də́zənt raɪt]

[hi ízənt ə tíčər]                   [ši də́zənt stə́di]

[ši ízənt ə tíčər]                   [ši də́zənt wərk]

[hi ízənt ə lóyər]                   [ši də́zənt it]

[ši ízənt ə lóyər]

[aɪm nat ə⌐daktər]                   [ðe wərnt⌐ízi]

[aɪm nat ə tíčər]                    [ðe wərnt dífıkəlt]

[aɪm nat ə lóyər]                    [ðe wərnt íntrıstıŋ]

[aɪm nat ə prəfɛ́sər]                [ðə wərnt gud]

[aɪm nat ə dɛ́ntıst]                 [ðe wərnt bæd]

[aɪm nat ə nərs]                     [ðe wərnt smɔl]

[hi dıdənt⌐rɪd]                      [ıt wə́zənt⌐ízi]

[hi dídənt raɪt]                     [ıt wə́zənt dífıkəlt]

[hi dídənt stə́di]                   [ıt wə́zənt íntrıstıŋ]

[hi dídənt wərk]                     [ıt wə́zənt gud]

[hi dídənt ǽnsər]                    [ıt wə́zənt bæd]

[hi dídənt it]                       [ıt wə́zənt smɔl]

---

[1] You will also frequently hear an extreme reduction of <u>going to</u> [gənə] in such a sentence as the following: [aɪm gənə stədi tənaɪt]

### 6. Change of vowel in unaccented syllable

Which is the loudest or accented syllable in definite? The first syllable, DE-finite. In explain? The last syllable, ex-PLAIN. In university? The third syllable, uni-V-ERsity. Notice that one syllable is always pronounced more loudly than the others in every word of more than one syllable.

The vowel in unaccented syllables is usually [ɪ], [ɛ], or [ə]. In some words the vowel in an unaccented syllable disappears. For example, comfortable, [kə́mftəbəl]; interesting, [íntrɪstɪŋ]; chocolate, [čɔ́klət].

Observe the pronunciations of the following words. Notice that the pronunciation of the accented syllables does not vary; notice that the vowels of the unaccented syllables are different.

| | | |
|---|---|---|
| [ɛksplén] | [défɪnɪt] | [yunɪvə́rsɪti] |
| [ɪksplén] | [défənət] | [yunəvə́rsəti] |

Two speakers often pronounce the same unaccented syllable differently, and one person often pronounces the same unaccented syllable differently on different occasions.

You will find many differences similar to those in the above words, but the quality of the accented vowels practically does not fluctuate.

# LESSON VI

## PRONUNCIATION

1. Pronunciation of [ə] and [a]
2. Pronunciation of [a] contrasted with [æ]
3. Pronunciation of [aɪ]
4. Pronunciation of [r] after consonants
5. Reduced forms of OUR, YOUR, HIS, HER
6. Rhythm
7. Emphasis by intonation

## Review

a) Review these conversations from memory.

1. Teacher A. Where is the man?
   Teacher B. He's in class.

2. Student A. Where is your room?
   Student B. It's near the Rackham Building.

b) Pronounce the following words. Notice that all the words in the list are regularly spelled with the letter a but pronounced [æ].

[æ]

| | | | | |
|---|---|---|---|---|
| bat | sat | lad | hat | lack |
| man | sad | slap | ask | back |
| pan | bad | mat | add | last |

c) Pronounce the following words. Notice that all the words in the list are regularly spelled with the letter e but pronounced [ɛ].

[ɛ]

| | | | | |
|---|---|---|---|---|
| bet | men | pen | set | bed |
| led | fed | met | net | red |
| less | pens | pets | bets | test |

d) Pronounce the following sentences making a contrast between the sounds [æ] and [ɛ].

| I said, " man." | I said, " lad." |
|---|---|
| men | led |
| bat | past |
| bet | pest |
| pan | last |
| pen | lest |
| bad | pans |
| bed | pens |

55

## 1. Pronunciation of [ə] contrasted with [a]

In the vowel [ə] the tongue position is <u>mid central</u>, and the lips are <u>unrounded</u>. This sound is pronounced with <u>tense</u> muscles in stressed syllables, it is pronounced with re-<u>laxed</u> muscles in unstressed syllables. Pronounce <u>come</u> [kəm] and <u>about</u> [əbaut].

In the vowel [a] the tongue position is <u>low central</u>. The muscles are <u>relaxed</u>. The tongue is farther back than for [æ] and lower than for [ə]. Notice the difference in tongue position for [ə] and [a] in the diagram.

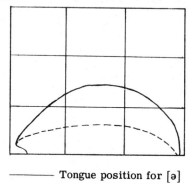

———————— Tongue position for [ə]

-------- Tongue position for [a]

Pronounce the following words. When the teacher tells you that your pronunciation is not exactly correct, move your tongue higher, lower, farther front, or farther back or make the sound longer in order to mimic the teacher exactly.

| 1 [ə] | 2 [a] |
|-------|-------|
| [səm] | [sam] |
| [sək] | [sak] |
| [pət] | [pat] |
| [kət] | [kat] |
| [hət] | [hat] |
| [lək] | [lak] |
| [nət] | [nat] |
| [kəp] | [kap] |

Pronounce the following pair of sentences:

1. There's a duck [dək].
2. There's a dock [dak].

Pronounce the following sentences:

[ɪts natʃhæt]

[hiz itɪŋʃlənč]

[aɪ laɪk ɪt vɛriʃməč]

Memorize the following conversations:

Doctor W.   [ar yəʃhəŋgri]

Doctor R.   [no aɪmʃnæt]

Doctor L.   [ar yəʃhəŋgri]

Doctor M.   [yɛs aɪm goɪŋ tə itʃlənč nau]

## 2. Pronunciation of [a] contrasted with [æ]

Notice the difference in tongue position for the sounds [a] and [æ].

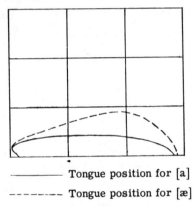

———————  Tongue position for [a]

— — — — —  Tongue position for [æ]

Pronounce the following words:

| 1 [a] | 2 [æ] |
|-------|-------|
| [sam] | [sæm] |
| [sak] | [sæk] |
| [pat] | [pæt] |
| [kat] | [kæt] |
| [hat] | [hæt] |
| [lak] | [læk] |
| [nat] | [næt] |
| [kap] | [kæp] |

Pronounce the following sentences:

[ðə mæn ɪz nat ∫həŋgri]

[ðə klæs bɪgɪnz æt et əklɑk]

[hi æsks mɛni ∫kwɛs t∫ənz]

Memorize the following conversation:

Tall man:    [aɪ want ə nu ∫hæt]

Short man:   [haʊ mət∫ məni du yə hæv]

Tall man:    [aɪ hæv faɪv dɑlərz]

Short man:   [ðæts nat ənəf lɛts go tə ðə bæŋk]

## 3. Pronunciation of [aɪ]

The tongue position changes during the pronunciation of [aɪ]. The tongue begins in the position for [a]. This sound is made very long. Then the tongue moves to the position for [ɪ]. The muscles are relaxed during the pronunciation of [aɪ].

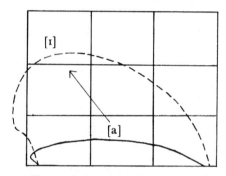

Change in tongue position for [aɪ]

Pronounce the following words and sentences:

| [faɪv] | [naɪn] | [taɪm] | [paɪp] | [baɪ] | [aɪm] |
| [laɪk] | [hwaɪt] | [raɪt] | [t∫aɪld] | [naɪf] | [waɪf] |

[ðə t∫aɪld ɪz baɪɪŋ səm aɪs krim]

[aɪm goɪŋ tə baɪ ə naɪf æn ə paɪp]

[hɪz waɪf ɪz baɪɪŋ səm hwaɪt pepər]

[ðə t∫aɪld ɪz faɪv yɪrz old]

Practice the following conversation:

Student A. [du yə hæv ̚raɪ̯tɪŋ pepər]

Student B. [yɛs hwət ̚kaɪnd ̚du yə ̚wɑnt]

Student A. [aɪ want səm ̚hwaɪt pepər]

## 4. Pronunciation of [r] after consonant

Pronounce [rum, rod, rid, rən, ræn] with rounded lips and without touching the tongue to the top of the mouth.

| [pəró] | [pəró] | [prə] |     | [bəró] | [bəró] | [brə] |
|--------|--------|-------|-----|--------|--------|-------|
| [kəró] | [kəró] | [krə] |     | [gəró] | [gəró] | [grə] |
| [təró] | [təró] | [trə] |     | [dəró] | [dəró] | [drə] |
| [spəró]| [spəró]| [sprə]|     | [stəró]| [stəró]| [strə]|

Pronounce the following words and sentences:

| [grin]  | [tri]  | [krim]  |     | [praɪs]  | [brəš] |
|---------|--------|---------|-----|----------|--------|
| [tren]  | [drɛs] | [strit] |     | [sprɪŋ]  | [tre]  |

[ə braun ̚drɛs]

[aɪs ̚krim]

[ši hæs ə braun ̚drɛs]

[ðə tri ɪz ̚grin]

[ə grin ̚tri]

[ə lɔŋ ̚strit]

[ɪz ðə ̚tren ̚hɪr]

[aɪ laɪk aɪs ̚krim]

Memorize the following conversations:

Student A. [hwət ̚kələr ɪz ər ̚drɛs]

Student B. [ɪts ̚braun]

Student A. [hwət ̚kələr ɪz ɪz ̚taɪ]

Student B. [ɪts ̚grin]

## 5. Reduced forms of OUR, YOUR, HIS, HER

Pronounce the following group of words:

[ðə mænz ɪn yər ̚haus]          The man's in your house.

[ðe nid ar ̚buks]               They need our books.

[hwəts ər ̚nem]                 What's her name?

[hwəts ɪz ̚nem]                 What's his name?

[hwəts yər ̚nem]                What's your name?

Notice the difference between the reduced form and the full form of the following words:

|      | Full Form | Reduced Form |
|------|-----------|--------------|
| our  | [aʊr]     | [ar]         |
| your | [yʊr]     | [yər]        |
| his  | [hɪz]     | [ɪz]         |
| her  | [hər]     | [ər]         |

Pronounce the following word groups and sentences with normal rapid pronunciation. Use the 2-4 intonation curve.

[ɪn ar⌐hàʊs]

[ɪn ər⌐rùm]

[rid ɪz⌐bʊ̀k]

[baɪ ər⌐brɛkfəst]

[sɪŋ ar⌐sɔ̀ŋ]

[tə ɪz⌐mə́ðər]

[frəm ər⌐fàðər]

[gɪv ɪz⌐hæ̀t]

[gɪv ar⌐hæ̀ts]

[šek ɪz⌐hæ̀nd]

[šek ər⌐hæ̀nd]

[hwəts ɪz⌐nèm]

[hwəts ər⌐nèm]

[hwɛrz ar⌐dìnər]

Practice the following conversations using the reduced forms of our, your, his, her.

    Lawyer A.  Are these _____ books?

           B.  Yes, they're _____ books.

  Secretary A.  Where's _____ class?

           B.  _____ class is in this building.

## 6. Rhythm

### Simple rhythm groups

English syllables are pronounced in groups, not separately.[1] A group of syllables pronounced together is called a rhythm group. Simple rhythm groups have one stressed syllable; several unstressed syllables may precede or follow the stressed syllable. The following are simple rhythm groups.

---

[1] Note to the teacher: Speakers of English generally unite more words in rhythm groups than speakers of Spanish. Spanish speakers need to learn to pronounce groups of words as units without separation into single words. Spanish speakers also need to learn to recognize the units in rapid speech. For the purpose of teaching this recognition the teacher should use normal rapid pronunciation in all conversation with the class. He should not try to "speak slowly and distinctly" nor separate his words so that the student "will understand more easily." If the teacher finds it necessary to separate words by slow speech, he should repeat the sentence with normal pronunciation.

[līst]                          [nǫ]

[ɪn̩trɪstɪŋ]                     [kwɛs̆t͡ʃənz]

[yunɪ̄vərˈsɪti]                  [rɪ̄mɛm̩bər]

Rhythm groups of several words are similar in stress and intonation to rhythm groups of single words. The length of time in the pronunciation of rhythm groups of several words is not necessarily longer than it is in the pronunciation of rhythm groups of single words. Observe the following rhythm groups. Pronounce them.

[ɛnĵɪ̆n̩r]

[ən ɛnĵɪ̆n̩r]

[ə gʊd ɛnĵɪ̆n̩r]

Notice that the amount of time consumed in pronouncing the first word is the same as that for the last group of words, even though more syllables have been added. Each simple rhythm group (as above) has one word which is being emphasized.

Pronounce the following groups of words in single rhythm groups; pronounce them as single words.

[ðɪ æftərˌnᷩn]                  [hæz ə⌐dɔ̀g]

[ðɪ ə̣drɛs]                     [hæz ə⌐hàʊs]

[ðɪ ɛksplə̣neš̆ən]              [hæz ə⌐sə̀n]

[ðɪ ɪntrə̣dək̆šən]              [aɪ əndərˈstænd⌐ɪm]

[ɪn ðə⌐hàʊs]                    [aɪ rɪ̄mɛmbər ɪm]

[ɪn ðə⌐bæ̀ŋk]                   [hwəts yər⌐nɛ̀m]

[ɪn ðə⌐postʔofɪs]              [hwɛrz ðə⌐b̆ɔ̀ɪ]

## Sentence rhythm

When rhythm groups are combined in sentences the alternate stressed and unstressed syllables and the alternate high and low pitches form a sentence rhythm. This sentence rhythm may be compared to a series of waves; each simple rhythm group is a separate wave.

The following diagram of sentence rhythm may clarify the preceding discussion. Observe the relation between the stresses in the sentences and the sentence rhythm.

[ðə prə̣f̆ɛsər⌐ti̊t͡ʃəz ðə⌐lɛ̆sən]

In sentence rhythm the stressed syllables tend to occur at relatively regular intervals and the waves are relatively uniform. This uniformity is preserved even when the number of syllables in each rhythm group varies. One rhythm group may contain five syllables; another group may contain one syllable; another may contain three syllables; but each group utilizes approximately the same amount of time. When a rhythm group contains many syllables, the syllables are spoken very rapidly, and they are often reduced in order to occupy the same amount of time as the preceding rhythm group. When a rhythm group contains only one syllable, the syllable is prolonged in order to occupy the same amount of time needed for other rhythm groups.[1]

Pronounce the following series of syllables. The teacher will indicate the speed of pronunciation by tapping with his pencil.[2] Read the horizontal columns; then read the vertical columns.

| lá | lá | lá |
|---|---|---|
| lalə | lalə | lalə |
| lə lalə | lə lalə | lə lalə |
| lalələlə | lalələlə | lalələlə |
| lə lalələ | lə lalələ | lə lalələ |

Read the following sentences with normal rapid pronunciation. Place the stresses at regular intervals. The teacher will indicate the speed by tapping with his pencil.[3]

[ɪŋglɪš ɪz izi]                        [ən ɪŋglɪš lɛsənz izi]

[ɪŋglɪš ɪz izi]                        [ən ɪŋglɪš lɛsənz izi]

[ɪŋglɪš ɪz izi]                        [ən ɪŋglɪš lɛsənz izi]

[ɪŋglɪš ɪz vɛri izi]                   [ən ɪŋglɪš lɛsənz vɛri izi]

[ɪŋglɪš ɪz vɛri izi]                   [ən ɪŋglɪš lɛsənz vɛri izi]

[ɪŋglɪš ɪz vɛri izi]                   [ən ɪŋglɪš lɛsənz vɛri izi]

---

[1] Spanish speakers often do not adjust the speed of syllables in rhythm groups in English in order to obtain good sentence rhythm. Spanish speakers need to practice the pronunciation of long rhythm groups in order to learn to pronounce them rapidly and adjust them to the sentence rhythm. They need to practice very short rhythm groups in order to learn to prolong them and adjust them to the sentence rhythm.

[2] Note to the teacher: Practice should begin slowly with about one tap per second. Once the students understand the drill, the speed can be increased to about one and one-half or two taps per second. Once the speed is established, maintain the same speed for the rest of the drills. Do not give extra time for extra syllables or the purpose of the drill is lost. Tap once for each rhythm group.

[3] If possible each student should work through all the sentences at one time. However, the entire class may pronounce the sentences in unison; this exercise helps to build up the pressure for speed. Read the sentences with normal rapid pronunciation. If the first sentence is read very rapidly it may be difficult to sustain the rhythm. Adjust the rhythm to the ability of the class but try to sustain a relatively normal rapidity.

## 7. Emphasis by intonation

Notice the following sentence.

The student speaks Spanish.

If the student speaks only one language, which word do you want to emphasize in the above sentence? Spanish. Notice the change in pitch on the word which you want to point out.

The student speaks Spanish.

If you want to show that the student doesn't read or write Spanish, which word do you want to emphasize? Speaks.

The student speaks Spanish.

Now you want to emphasize the person who speaks Spanish. Which word do you point out? Student.

The student speaks Spanish.

In this manner you can emphasize any word in the sentence by using the 2-4 intonation curve.

Pronounce the following sentences:

[ðə studənt spiks spænɪš]

[ɪts ə blu drɛs]

[huz həŋgri aɪm həŋgri]

[hiz hɪr bət šiz nat]

Notice that the pitch of the unstressed syllables is low. When the pitch is low on unstressed syllables, more emphasis is given to the syllables with high pitch.

[ðə bɔɪ laɪks kændi]

[ðə bɔɪ laɪks kændi]

[ðə bɔɪ laɪks kændi]

[ðə bɔɪ laɪks kændi]

Notice that the intonation curve begins on the stressed syllable. The 2-4 intonation curve is used in order to give emphasis or in order to indicate a contrast.

Practice the following conversations with contrasting emphasis:

Doctor Y.   How are you?

Doctor X.   Just fine, thank you.  How are you?

Doctor Y.   Very well, thank you.


Student A.   What are you doing?

Student B.   I'm reading.  What are you doing?

Student A.   I'm studying English.

# LESSON VII

## PRONUNCIATION

1. Pronunciation of [u] and [ʊ]
2. Pronunciation of [ʊ] contrasted with [ə]
3. Pronunciation of [aʊ]
4. Rhythm drills
5. Reduced forms of HIM, HER, THEM
6. The spelling alphabet

Review

a) Review these conversations from memory.

| | |
|---|---|
| Doctor W. | Are you hungry? |
| Doctor R. | No, I'm not. |

| | |
|---|---|
| Tall man. | I want a new hat. |
| Short man. | How much money do you have? |
| Tall man. | I have five dollars. |
| Short man. | That's not enough. Let's go to the bank. |

| | |
|---|---|
| Student A. | What color is his tie? |
| Student B. | It's green. |

| | |
|---|---|
| Doctor Y. | How are you? |
| Doctor X. | Just fine, thank you. How are you? |
| Doctor Y. | Very well, thank you. |

b) Pronounce the following words. Notice that all the words in the list are regularly spelled with the letter o but pronounced [a].

### [a]

| | | | | |
|---|---|---|---|---|
| cot | lot | cop | sock | rock |
| not | pot | stop | dock | clock |
| hot | Tom | lock | John | stock |

c) Pronounce the following words. Notice that all the words in the list are regularly spelled with the letter u but pronounced [ə].

### [ə]

| | | | | |
|---|---|---|---|---|
| cup | mud | cut | luck | cups |
| hut | but | bus | truck | stuck |
| sun | nut | duck | dust | suck |

d) Pronounce the following words. Notice that all the words in the list are regularly spelled with the letter a but pronounced [æ].

| | | | | |
|---|---|---|---|---|
| cap | pat | fat | sack | last |
| bat | hat | sad | black | fast |
| cat | rat | tap | pass | ask |

64

e) Pronounce the following sentences making a contrast between the sounds [a], [ə], and [æ].[1]

|               |       |   | I see the | cup.  |
|---------------|-------|---|-----------|-------|
| John has a    | cot.  |   |           | cap   |
|               | dock  |   |           | cop   |
|               | sock  |   |           | dock  |
|               | lock  |   |           | duck  |
| John has a    | cup.  |   |           | truck |
|               | cut   |   |           | track |
|               | bus   |   |           | hut   |
|               | truck |   |           | hat   |
| John has a    | cap.  |   |           | stock |
|               | bat   |   |           | stack |
|               | cat   |   |           |       |
|               | hat   |   |           |       |

## 1. Pronunciation of [u] and [ʊ]

In the vowel [u] the tongue position is <u>high back</u>; the lips are <u>rounded</u>, and the muscles are <u>tense</u>. Pronounce [rum].

In the pronunciation of the vowel [ʊ] the tongue position is <u>high back</u>; the lips are <u>slightly rounded</u>, and the muscles are <u>relaxed</u>. Pronounce [fʊt].

Notice the difference in tongue position for [u] and [ʊ].

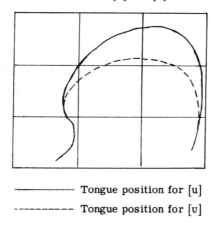

——————— Tongue position for [u]

- - - - - - - Tongue position for [ʊ]

---

[1] Note to the teacher: It often helps if the student is told to make the [a] sound very long.

Pronounce the following words:

| 1 [u]   | 2 [ʊ]   |
|---------|---------|
| [ful]   | [fʊl]   |
| [luk]   | [lʊk]   |
| [sut]   | [sʊt]   |
| [kud]   | [kʊd]   |

Pronounce the following pair of sentences.

Luke [luk], come here.

Look [lʊk], come here.

Pronounce the following words and sentences containing the sound [u].

| [rum]   | [grup]  | [tuθ]   | [blu]   | [æftərnún] |
|---------|---------|---------|---------|------------|
| [šu]    | [nu]    | [fud]   | [spun]  | [ču]       |

[hi hæz ə nu⌐rum]                     [hwɛr ɪz yər⌐rum]

[ðə nu grup ɪz⌐hɪr]                    [ðɪs ɪz ə nu⌐sut]

Pronounce the following words and sentences containing the sound [ʊ].

| [gʊd]   | [pʊt]    | [lʊk]   | [fʊt]   | [bʊk]   |
|---------|----------|---------|---------|---------|
| [kʊd]   | [šúgər]  | [tʊk]   | [fʊl]   | [šʊk]   |

[ɪz ðə bʊk⌐gʊd]                        [hwɛr ɪz ðə⌐šʊgər]

[ðə bʊk ɪz vɛri⌐gʊd]                   [ðə šugər ɪz an ðə⌐tebəl]

Memorize the following conversations:

Student A. [ɪz ðə fud⌐gʊd]

Student B. [yɛs ðə fud ɪz⌐gʊd]

Student A. [ɪz ðə fud⌐gʊd]

Student B. [no ðə fud ɪzənt⌐gʊd]

## 2. Pronunciation of [ʊ] contrasted with [ə]

Notice the difference in tongue position of the sounds [ʊ] and [ə] in the following diagram. The lips are rounded in the pronunciation of [ʊ] and they are not rounded in the pronunciation of [ə].

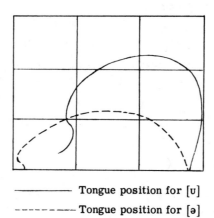

——————— Tongue position for [ʊ]

- - - - - - - - Tongue position for [ə]

Pronounce the following words.

| 1 [ʊ] | 2 [ə] |
|-------|-------|
| [kʊd] | [kəd] |
| [stʊd] | [stəd] |
| [lʊk] | [lək] |
| [tʊk] | [tək] |
| [bʊk] | [bək] |

Practice the following conversation:

Student A. [dʊ yə laɪk ðə ʃbʊk]

Student B. [yɛs aɪ laɪk ɪt vɛri ʃməč]

## 3. Pronunciation of [aʊ]

In the dipthong [aʊ] the tongue begins in the position for [a]; the tongue is in low central position and the lips are unrounded. During the sound the tongue rises to a high back position and the lips are rounded.

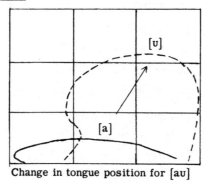

Change in tongue position for [aʊ]

Pronounce the following words:

[haʊs]        [braʊn]        [aʊt]        [prənaúns]        [naʊ]

[kaʊ]        [haʊ məč]        [saʊnd]        [blaʊs]        [daʊn]

Pronounce the following phrases with normal rapid pronunciation. Distinguish particularly between [ʊ], [aʊ], and [u].

[ɪn ðə haʊs]                    [wɪðaʊt ə daʊt]

[ɪn ðə grʊp]                    [wɪðaʊt fʊd]

[ɪn ðə bʊk]                    [wɪðaʊt wʊl]

[ɪn ðə wʊl]                    [wɪðaʊt šugər]

[ðə braʊn haʊs]                [ə paʊnd əv šugər]

[ðə pʊr kaʊ]                    [ən aʊns əv wʊl]

[ðə gʊd fʊd]                    [ə paʊnd əv frʊt]

[ðə gʊd šugər]                [ə gʊd blaʊs]

[haʊ məč ɪz ðə bʊk]

[haʊ məč ɪz ðə blaʊs]

[haʊ məč ɪz ðə šugər]

[haʊ məč ɪz ðə wʊl]

## 4. Rhythm drills

Read the following sentences. The teacher will indicate the speed of pronunciation. Read each sentence three times.

[ðə daktərz ə studənt]

[ðə daktərz ə gʊd studənt]

[ðə daktərz ə vɛri gʊd studənt]

[ðə nu daktərz ə vɛri gʊd studənt]

[ðə nu daktərz nat ə vɛri gʊd studənt]

[hi siz ðə bʊk]

[hi siz ðə smɔl bʊk]

[hi notɪsɪz ðə smɔl bʊk]

[dəz hi notɪs ðə vɛri smɔl bʊk]

[ðɪ onər əv ðə stɔr]

[aɪm ðɪ onər əv ðə stɔr]

[aɪm nat ðɪ onər əv ðə stɔr]

[aɪm nat ðɪ onər əv ə vɛri larǰ stɔr]

5. Reduced forms of HIM, HER, THEM

Pronounce the following sentences.

[aɪ si ɪm]                          I see him.

[hi pez ðəm]                        He pays them.

[wi no ər]                          We know her.

Notice the difference between the reduced form and the full form of the following words:

|       | Full form | Reduced form |
|-------|-----------|--------------|
| him   | [hɪm]     | [ɪm]         |
| her   | [hər]     | [ər]         |
| them  | [ðɛm]     | [ðəm] or [əm] |

Pronounce the following phrases and sentences with normal rapid pronunciation. Use the 2-4 intonation.

[yu no ɪm]                          [mɪstər wɪlsən noz ər]

[wi want əm]                        [ðə tičər laɪks ɪm]

[wi tek ðəm]                        [hi noz ðəm]

[ðe laɪk ər]                        [aɪ rɪmɛmbər ər]

[hi hɛlps ɪm]                       [wi mit ɪm]

Practice the following conversation:

Student A.  [dəz ðə tičər no ər]

Student B.  [yɛs hi noz ər]

Substitute him and them in the above conversation.

## 6. The spelling alphabet

| Letter of the Spelling Alphabet | Name of the Letter | Letter of the Spelling Alphabet | Name of the Letter |
|:---:|:---:|:---:|:---:|
| a | [e] | n | [ɛn] |
| b | [bi] | o | [o] |
| c | [si] | p | [pi] |
| d | [di] | q | [kyu] |
| e | [i] | r | [ar] |
| f | [ɛf] | s | [ɛs] |
| g | [ʃi] | t | [ti] |
| h | [eč] | u | [yu] |
| i | [aɪ] | v | [vi] |
| j | [ʃe] | w | [dəbəlyu] |
| k | [ke] | x | [ɛks] |
| l | [ɛl] | y | [waɪ] |
| m | [ɛm] | z | [zi] |

Spell aloud the following words:

| | | |
|---|---|---|
| teacher | January | English |
| hospital | explain | conversation |
| envelope | zero | understand |
| friend | frequent | brown |
| king | examination | year |

What are the names of these letters?

| | | |
|---|---|---|
| g | q | a |
| j | y | e |
| k | z | i |

# LESSON VIII

## PRONUNCIATION

1. Pronunciation of [o] and [ɔ]
2. Pronunciation of [ɔ] contrasted with [ə]
3. Pronunciation of [ɔɪ]
4. Pronunciation of irregular past forms of class 2 words

Review

a) Review these conversations from memory.

    1. Student A. Is the food good?

       Student B. Yes, the food is good.

    2. Lawyer A. Are these your books?

       Lawyer B. Yes, they're my books.

(Substitute our, his, her, for your, in the above conversation.)

b) Spell your name in the English alphabet.

c) What are the names of these letters? i, e, u, w, v, b, k, g, j, o, y, a.

1. Pronunciation of [o] and [ɔ]

    In the vowel [o] the tongue position is mid back, the lips are rounded, and the muscles are tense. During the sound [o] the tongue is raised to the high back position. This change in position causes the vowel to be slightly diphthongized.[1] Pronounce go [go].

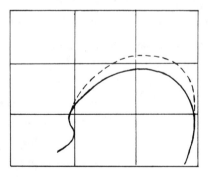

Change in tongue position for [o]

---

[1] Note to the teacher: If one wishes to symbolize the diphthongization he can indicate the sound by the symbol [oᵁ]. This can be used during the first period in teaching this sound because it helps to remind the student of the gliding quality in this vowel.

71

In the pronunciation of [ɔ] the tongue position is <u>low back</u>, the lips are slightly <u>rounded</u>, and the muscles are <u>tense</u>. Pronounce <u>dog</u> [dɔg].

Notice the difference in tongue position for the sounds [o] and [ɔ].

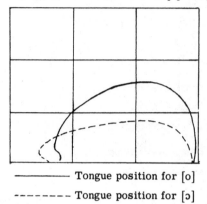

——————— Tongue position for [o]

------- Tongue position for [ɔ]

Pronounce the following words:

| 1 [o] | 2 [ɔ] |
|-------|-------|
| [lo] | [lɔ] |
| [fol] | [fɔl] |
| [bot] | [bɔt] |
| [not] | [nɔt] |
| [kold] | [kɔld] |
| [kot] | [kɔt] |
| [tost] | [tɔst] |
| [kol] | [kɔl] |

Pronounce the following word groups and sentences.

[o]

[notɪs ɪt]                         [ə bol əv frut]

[opən ɪt]                          [ðə sut ɪz old]

[kloz ɪt]                          [ðə kot ɪz nu]

[smok ɪt]                          [ðə rum ɪz old]

[hold ɪt]                          [pliz kloz ðə windo]

[aɪ dont no]                       [hi hæz ən old bot]

[ɪn ðə kɔfi]                       [aɪ sɔ ðə sɔlt]

[ɪn ðə kɔrnər]                     [aɪ sɔ ðə fɔrk]

[ɪn ðɪ ɔfɪs]                       [aɪ sɔ ðə fud]

[ɪn ðə ˈmɔrnɪŋ]                    [aɪ sɔ ðə ˈkɔfi]

[ɪn ðə ˈfɔl]                      [hiz ɪn ðɪ ˈɔfɪs]

[ɪn ðə ˈstɔr]                     [hi bɔt səm ˈkɔfi]

Memorize the following conversation:

Wife.       [aɪ bɔt ə nu ˈkɔt]

Husband.  [haʊ məč dɪd ɪt ˈkɔst]

Wife.       [ɪt kɔst fɔrti ˈdɑlərz]

## 2. Pronunciation of [ɔ] contrasted with [ə]

In the pronunciation of [ɔ] the lips are <u>lightly rounded</u>; in [ə] they are <u>unrounded</u>.[1] Notice the difference in tongue position between these two sounds.

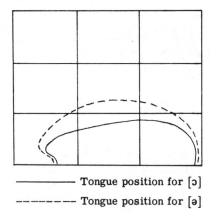

——————— Tongue position for [ɔ]

– – – – – – Tongue position for [ə]

Pronounce the following words:

| 1 [ɔ] | 2 [ə] |
|---|---|
| [bɔt] | [bət] |
| [kɔt] | [kət] |
| [kɔl] | [kəl] |
| [fɔn] | [fən] |
| [sɔŋ] | [səŋ] |
| [čɔk] | [čək] |

---

[1] Note to the teacher: Spanish speakers have a tendency to round the lips in pronouncing [ə]. A special attempt should be made to emphasize the difference in lip rounding between these two sounds.

Pronounce the following sentences:

[hiz ⌐stədiɪŋ]          [ši ⌐tɔks ǝ lat]

[hiz ⌐kǝmɪŋ]          [ðǝ bǝtǝr ⌐kɔst ǝ lat]

[hiz ⌐kɔlɪŋ]          [ðǝ bǝs ɪz ⌐hɪr]

[hiz ⌐tɔkɪŋ]          [aɪ lɔst ðǝ ⌐mǝni]

Memorize the following conversation:

Engineer A. [aɪ bɔt ǝ ⌐kar yɛstǝrdɪ]

Engineer B. [hau mǝč ⌐mǝni du yǝ hæv ⌐nau]

Engineer A. [nǝ̀n]

## 3. Pronunciation of [ɔɪ]

In the pronunciation of [ɔɪ] the tongue begins in a <u>low back</u> position. It then rises and moves forward to a <u>high front</u> position. The first part of the diphthong is pronounced for a longer time than the second part. Pronounce boy [bɔɪ]. The following diagram indicates the change in tongue position during the sound [ɔɪ].

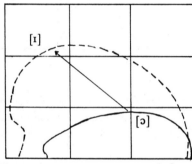

Change in tongue position for [ɔɪ]

Pronounce the following words and groups and groups of words.

[bɔɪ]          [ɛmplɔɪ]          [ɛnǰɔɪ]          [pɔɪnt]

[ðǝ bɔɪ ɪz ⌐kǝmɪŋ]          [ɛnǰɔɪ ðǝ ⌐fud]

[ðǝ bɔɪ ɪz ⌐itɪŋ]          [ɛnǰɔɪ ðǝ ⌐sɔŋz]

[ðǝ bɔɪ ɪz ⌐pleɪŋ]          [ɛnǰɔɪ ðǝ ⌐muviz]

[ðǝ bɔɪ ɪz ⌐sɪŋɪŋ]          [ɛnǰɔɪ ðǝ ⌐kansǝrts]

[ðǝ bɔɪ ɪz ⌐gɔɪŋ]          [ɛnǰɔɪ ðǝ ⌐klæsɪz]

Practice the following conversation.

Teacher. [dɪd yǝ ɛnǰɔɪ ðǝ ⌐muvi]

Student. [yɛ̀s aɪ ɛnǰɔɪd ⌐ɪt]

4. Pronunciation of irregular past forms of class 2 words (arranged as in the vowel chart)

Pronounce the following words. Pay particular attention to the vowel sounds as shown.

| | | | | |
|---|---|---|---|---|
| [ɪ] | did | | knew<br>(put)<br>took<br>(stood)<br>understood<br>shook | [u]<br><br>[ʊ] |
| [e]<br><br>[ɛ] | (came)<br>made<br>ate<br>(gave)<br><br>spent  said<br>left  (went)<br>felt  (met)<br>read<br>sent | [ə]<br>(was) | spoke<br>(told)<br>wrote<br>sold | [o] |
| [æ] | had<br>drank<br>sang<br>(sat) | got<br>forgot | bought<br>brought<br>(cost)<br>saw<br>taught<br>thought | [ɔ] |

[a]

Practice this exercise with the class 2 words from the chart not enclosed in parentheses.

Exercise:

Teacher: I do it.

Student: I did it.

## LESSON IX

### PRONUNCIATION

1. Pronunciation of [ər]
2. Review of the pronunciation of [r] in all positions
3. Review of [s], [z], and [ɪz] endings on class 1 and class 2 words
4. Pronunciation of irregular plurals of class 1 words
5. Practice on reduced forms
6. Practice on rhythm

### 1. Pronunciation of [ər]

The sound [ər] is like a vowel. Pronounce the sound [ə]. Raise only the tip of your tongue. Do not touch the top of your mouth with your tongue. Keep the middle of the tongue in the position for the sound [ə]. Round your lips slightly when you pronounce [ər].

Pronounce the following syllables in contrast.[1]

[ə]     [ər]     [ə]     [ər]     [ə]     [ər]     [ə]     [ər]     [ə]     [ər]

Pronounce the following words.

|  1 [ə]  |  2 [ər]  |
|---------|----------|
| [bən]   | [bərn]   |
| [bəd]   | [bərd]   |
| [bəg]   | [bərg]   |
| [šət]   | [šərt]   |
| [kət]   | [kərt]   |
| [tən]   | [tərn]   |

In order to learn to round your lips in pronouncing [ər] practice the following phrases. Do not stop between the [ər] sound and the [r] sound which follows. Practice the following.

[ər-ru] [2]      [ər-ru]      [ər-ru]      [ər-ru]

---

[1] Note to the teacher: These two sounds are contrasted here not because they are confused by Spanish-speakers but because an attempt is being made to retain the same position of the middle of the tongue in both sounds while adding the retroflex [r] to produce [ər]. Spanish-speakers have a strong tendency to pronounce this sound [ər] by raising and fronting the tongue, producing a sound similar to [ɛr]. Likewise in such words as word, learn, girl, etc. the students have a tendency to give the spelling pronunciation.

[2] Note to the teacher: Students often retain the lip rounding after they have pronounced [r]. This results in the sequence [ruid]. This tendency can be averted by having students practice unrounding their lips immediately after pronouncing the [r] sound to produce [rid].

76

[ðə tičər ˈrˌdz]¹                         [ðə daktər ˈrˌdz]

[ðə tičər raɪts]                          [ðə daktər raɪts]

[ðə tičər rənz]                           [ðə daktər rənz]

[ðə tičər rot]                            [ðə daktər rot]

[ðə tičər rɛd]                            [ðə daktər rɛd]

[maɪ faðər rot ə lɛtər]

[maɪ brəðər rot ə lɛtər]

[maɪ məðər rot ə lɛtər]

[maɪ sɪstər rot ə lɛtər]

[maɪ tičər rot ə lɛtər]

Pronounce the following words and sentences. Pay particular attention to the [ər] sound. If the teacher tells you that your pronunciation is not acceptable move your tongue into different positions until you can produce the sound satisfactorily.

| [wər] | [šərt] | [bétər] | [sístər] |
|---|---|---|---|
| [wərk] | [bərd] | [dɪzərt] | [kávər] |
| [lərn] | [fərst] | [ænsər] | [lɛkčər] |
| [gərl] | [tərn] | [bétər] | [əndərstænd] |

1. [ðə gərl ɪz wɛrɪŋ ə fər kot]

2. [hiz goɪŋ tə čərč]

3. [ðə gərl ɪz lərnɪŋ ðə wərdz]

4. [ɪts nɛvər tu let tə lərn]

5. [təde ɪz θərzdi]

6. [ðə prəfɛsər wəz ərli]

7. [ðə lɛtər ɪz əndər ðə bʊk]

8. [ðə tičər gev ə lɛkčər]

9. [ðə wərdz wər izi tə rɪmɛmbər]

10. [ðə wərk wəz izi]

---

¹Note to the teacher: In groups of sentences such as these in which the intonation is marked on the first sentence the other sentences should be pronounced with stress on the word in the same position within the sentence, e.g. [ðə tičər ˈrˌdz], [ðə tičər ˈraɪts], etc.

Memorize the following conversation.

Teacher: [dɪd yə‿lərn‿ðə nu‿wɚrdz]

Student: [yɛs aɪ‿lərnd‿ðəm‿yɛstərdi]

## 2. Review of the pronunciation of [r] in all positions

### [r] after vowels[1]

The tip of the tongue turns up toward the palate and the lips are slightly rounded. The voiced sound is continuous from the vowel sound to the [r] sound which follows it.

Pronounce the following:

| | | | |
|---|---|---|---|
| [fɔrk] | [farm] | [fɔrm] | [yard] |
| [kar] | [čɛr] | [larǰ] | [far] |
| [tíčər] | [kórnər] | [gárdən] | [hɪr] |

[ðə‿kar‿ɪz nɪr ðə‿hàus]

### [r] before vowels[2]

At the beginning of the sound [r], the tip of the tongue is turned up sharply toward the palate and the lips are rounded. Voicing begins and the tip of the tongue lowers to produce the vowel which follows [r]; the voiced sound is continuous during the pronunciation of [r] and the vowel which follows [r].

Pronounce the following:

| | | | |
|---|---|---|---|
| [rud] | [raɪt] | [rot] | [rɛd] |
| [raʊnd] | [rɔŋ] | [rid] | [rum] |
| [ráɪtɪŋ] | [rídɪŋ] | [róstɪŋ] | [ráɪdɪŋ] |

[aɪm‿rídɪŋ æn‿raɪtɪŋ ɪŋglɪš]

### [r] after consonants[3]

After stop sounds - [p, t, k, b, d, g] - in the same syllable, [r] is almost voiceless and slightly fricative. Do not touch the tooth ridge or the palate with the tongue.

Pronounce the following:

| | | | |
|---|---|---|---|
| [drɛs] | [braʊn] | [tri] | [drɪŋk] |
| [grin] | [tru] | [gro] | [gret] |
| [tren] | [praɪs] | [traɪ] | [pruv] |

[ðə drɛs ɪz‿grìn]

---

[1] For a fuller explanation, diagram, and exercises, see Lesson IV.

[2] For a fuller explanation and exercises see Lesson V.

[3] For a fuller explanation and exercises see Lesson VI.

Practice the following sentences. Remember that the tongue does not contact or vibrate against the tooth ridge or palate when you pronounce [r] correctly.

What is he reading?                    He's reading a book.

What is she reading?                   She's reading a book.
What are they reading?                 They're reading a book.
What are you reading?                  I'm reading a book.


What is he writing?                    He's writing some letters.

What is she writing?                   She's writing some letters.
What are they writing?                 They're writing some letters.
What are you writing?                  I'm writing some letters.


What is he wearing?                    He's wearing a green suit.

What is she wearing?                   She's wearing a green suit.
What are they wearing?                 They're wearing green suits.
What are you wearing?                  I'm wearing a green suit.


Where is he?                           He's in the garden.

Where is she?                          She's in the garden.
Where are they?                        They're in the garden.

3. Review of [s], [z], and [ɪz] endings on class 1 and class 2 words[1]

Pronounce the following sentences using the appropriate forms:

| The student_  are here. | The table_  are here. |
|---|---|
| doctor_ | chair_ |
| teacher_ | book_ |
| lawyer_ | hat_ |
| nurse_ | glove_ |
| professor_ | watch_ |
| boy_ | blouse_ |
| girl_ | sock_ |
| secretary_ | paper_ |
| engineer_ | pen_ |

---

[1] For a fuller explanation and exercises see Lesson II.

Pronounce the following sentences using the appropriate forms.

She wear_ a green hat.                    He teach_ the lesson.
She like_ ice cream.                      He send_ the letter.
She use_ a pen.                           He pay_ for the coffee.
She talk_ very much.                      He remember_ the words.
She go_ to the movies.                    He buy_ books.
She want_ to go to New York.              He discuss_ the lesson.
She discuss_ politics.                    He understand_ the movies.
She live_ in Ann Arbor.                   He like_ to go to the library.
She stud_ English.                        He wear_ a new suit.
She understand_ English.                  He sing_ a song.

## 4. Pronunciation of irregular plurals of class 1 words

Pronounce the following words. Notice the change in vowel sounds as shown.

| [u]  | tooth | [i]  | teeth    |
|------|-------|------|----------|
| [ʊ]  | foot  | [i]  | feet     |
| [aɪ] | child | [ɪ]  | children |
| [ʊ]  | woman | [ɪ]  | women    |
| [æ]  | man   | [ɛ]  | men      |

Pronounce the following words. Notice the change in consonant sounds.

| [f]  | wife  | [v]  | wives    |
|------|-------|------|----------|
| [f]  | knife | [v]  | knives   |

Pronounce the following words. Notice that there is no change in pronunciation between the two forms even though the spelling is different.

policeman [pəlísmən] policemen

gentleman [ʤɛ́ntəlmən] gentlemen

Use the correct form of the words in parentheses:

1. His (tooth) are white.

2. The (child) are playing.

3. The (woman) studied last night.

4. Her (foot) are small.

5. All of the (wife) are eating dinner.

6. The (knife) are on the table.

7. The (man) are doctors.

## 5. Practice on reduced forms

Pronounce the following phrases with normal rapid pronunciation. Use the 2-4 intonation.

[hiz ə stüdənt]            [šiz ə stüdənt]

[hiz ə tičər]             [šiz ə tičər]

[hiz ə daktər]            [šiz ə daktər]

[wɪr stüdənts]            [yur ə stüdənt]

[wɪr tičərz]              [yur ə tičər]

[wɪr daktərz]             [yur ə daktər]

[aɪm ə stüdənt]           [ðɛr stüdənts]

[aɪm ə tičər]             [ðɛr tičərz]

[aɪm ə daktər]            [ðɛr daktərz]

[aɪm ə kyübən]            [šiz ə brəzɪlyən]

[hiz ə kyübən]            [aɪm ə kyübən]

[šiz ə kyübən]            [yur ə mɛksɪkən]

[ɪts ə sɛntəns]           [ɪts ə haus]

[ɪts ə læŋgwɪǰ]           [ɪts ə bük]

[ɪts ə lɛtər]             [ɪts ə kwɛsčən]

[ɪts ə stæmp]             [ɪts ə rüm]

[ɪts ən ɛnvəlop]          [ɪts ə dɛsk]

[ɪts ə blækbɔrd]          [ɪts ə læmp]

[ɪts ə wɔl]               [ɪts ən əsaɪnmənt]

[hiz gɪvɪŋ ɪm ə bük]      [ɪz i gɪvɪŋ ər ə bük]

[hiz gɪvɪŋ ər ə bük]      [ɪz i gɪvɪŋ ɪm ə bük]

[hiz gɪvɪŋ ðəm ə bük]     [ɪz i gɪvɪŋ ðəm ə bük]

[hiz gɪvɪŋ yu ə bük]      [ɪz i gɪvɪŋ yu ə bük]

## 6. Practice on rhythm

Pronounce the following sentences with uniform rhythm.

[ðə | haʊs | wəz bɪsaɪd | ðə | bæŋk]

[ðə prəfɛsər | tiʧɪz ðə | lɛsən]

[hi | wanʧɪd tə | go | tə ðə | haʊs]

[ðə | gərl | ɪn maɪ | klæs | ɪz | prɪti]

[aɪ | want | tə | go | tə ðə | haʊs]

[ðe | want | tə | si | ðə | kæmpəs]

[hi | wants | tə | spik | wɪð | ʃan]

[ši | wants | tə | kæš | ə | ʧɛk]

[ðə | mɛn | ɪn ðə | haʊs | dont | no]

[ðə | bɔɪ | ət ðə | dɛsk | ɪz | stədiɪŋ]

[du yə | no ðə | bɔɪ | ɪn ðə | stɔr]

[wəz ðə | studənt | ɪn | klæs | an | məndɪ]

## PRONUNCIATION

1. Review of vowels: vowel rhymes
2. Review of the forms of class 2 words
3. Practice on 2-4 intonation
4. Rhythm drills
5. Pronunciation practice with pictures

## 1. Review of vowels

Pronounce the following sentences:

(a) I see the cup.
cap
sheep
ship
pen
pan
ball
bowl
pin
pen

(b) He said low.
law
coal
call
led
lid
meet
met
nut
not

(c) He's leaving.
living
sleeping
slipping

(d) He said "came."
come
comb
sail
sell
Luke
look
luck
fool
full

(e) I need money.
many

(f) He's hungry.
angry.

83

Vowel rhymes

Choose the word in parenthesis that contains the same vowel sound as the last word in the first line.  Write it in the space provided and pronounce the rhyme.

1. Do you really believe
   That he's going to _____          1. (liv, lɪv)

2. How much will you give
   To have the dog _____             2. (liv, lɪv)

3. If Mary will wait
   We won't make her _____           3. (let, lɛt)

4. I hope you won't tell
   That I don't want to _____         4. (sel, sɛl)

5. She wore a red pin
   That was made out of _____            5. (tɛn, tɪn)

6. The law doesn't let
   A man make a _____                6. (bɛt, bɪt)

7. Look at that rat
   He's gone after the _____          7. (kat, kæt)

8. You may drink it or not
   I don't think it's too _____        8. (hat, hæt)

9. I would use my knife, but
   I'm not sure it will _____          9. (kæt, kət)

10. He's not good in school
    People call him a _____           10. (ful, fʊl)

## 2. Review of the forms of class 2 words

a) Use the past forms of the words in parentheses in the following sentences.

Example:  They (speak) spoke English.

1. The students (come) _____ to the university.
2. They (see) _____ many buildings on the campus.
3. The boys (buy) _____ some paper at the bookstore.
4. They (go) _____ to class at eight o'clock.
5. They (take) _____ their books with them.
6. (Do) _____ they understand the teachers?
7. The teachers (speak) _____ very slowly.
8. They (teach) _____ them many things about English.
9. All of the students (read) _____ and (understand) _____ the lessons.
10. The teachers and students (leave) _____ the class-room at two o'clock.

b) Use the appropriate form of the words in parentheses in the following sentences.

Example: He (like) <u>likes</u> English.

      1. The boy (study) _____ English.
      2. He (like) _____ it very much.
      3. He (walk) _____ to class in the morning.
      4. He (talk) _____ to his friends in the class-room.
      5. He (open) _____ the book and (pronounce) _____ the words.
      6. He (repeat) _____ the sentences.
      7. He (answer) _____ all of the questions.
      8. He sometimes (ask) _____ questions.
      9. He (want) _____ to learn English well.
    10. He (work) _____ very hard in class.

c) Use the past form of the words in parentheses in the sentences in section b.

Example: He (like) <u>liked</u> English.

3. Practice on 2-4 intonation

a) Practice the following sentences using 2-4 intonation.

      1. She understands the question.

      2. The magazines are very interesting.

      3. Where are the students?

      4. John is coming to Ann Arbor.

      5. Is he a doctor?

      6. When do we eat dinner?

      7. The boy liked the food yesterday.

      8. How much did the book cost?

      9. The women received many letters.

    10. We usually attend the concerts.

b) The teacher will tell you to emphasize different words in these sentences. Pronounce the sentences with 2-4 intonation on the words which the teacher tells you.

Example:
    Teacher.    under<u>stands</u>

    Student.    She under<u>stands</u> the question.

4. Rhythm drills

Pronounce these sentences. Pay particular attention to the pronunciation of <u>him</u>, <u>his</u>, <u>her</u>, <u>them</u>, <u>their</u>, <u>you</u>, <u>your</u>.

[ ðə mæn laɪks ər]
        ɪm
        əm

[ ðə bɔɪ hɛlps ər]
        ɪm
        əm

[ ðə gərl rɪmɛmbərz ər]
        ɪm
        əm

[ mɪstər braun noz ər]
        ɪm
        əm

[ ðə gərlz lʊkɪŋ æt ɪm ]
    spikɪŋ tu ɪm
    tɔkɪŋ tu ɪm
    læfɪŋ æt ɪm

[ ðə bɔɪz lʊkɪŋ æt ər]
        ɪm
        əm

[ ðə bɔɪz tɔkɪŋ tu ɪm ]
        ər
        əm

[ ðə bɔɪz læfɪŋ æt ɪm ]
        ər
        əm

[ ðə bɔɪz spikɪŋ tu ər]
        ɪm
        əm

[ ðə tičərz læfɪŋ æt əm ]
    tɔkɪŋ tu əm
    lʊkɪŋ æt əm
    spikɪŋ tu əm

5. Pronunciation practice with pictures[1]

Give the name of the object or activity in the pictures below.

---

[1] Note to the teacher: This is an exercise for the practice on the [r] sound. The objects or activities can be named or talked about. The words to be elicited are: <u>tree</u>, <u>dress</u>, <u>tray</u>, <u>three</u>, <u>reading</u>, <u>writing</u>, <u>ice cream</u>, <u>street</u>.

## LESSON XI

## PRONUNCIATION

1. Review of [i], [ɪ], [u], [ʊ]
2. Consonant formation in general
3. Flexibility of the organs of speech
4. Pronunciation of [t] between vowels
5. Drill on length of vowels before voiced consonants
6. Pronunciation of CAN and CAN'T
7. Smooth sentence rhythm

## 1. Review of [i], [ɪ], [u], [ʊ]

a) Pronounce the following sentences in rapid alternation.

    1. [aɪ ⌐bit⌐ ɪt]    I beat it.

    2. [aɪ ⌐bɪt⌐ ɪt]    I bit it.

Pronounce the following pairs of words:

| | |
|---|---|
| [grin] | [grɪn] |
| [sin] | [sɪn] |
| [rid] | [rɪd] |
| [tik] | [tɪk] |
| [liv] | [lɪv] |
| [fil] | [fɪl] |

b) Pronounce the following sentence:

    [hi hæd ⌐sʊt⌐ an ɪz ⌐sut]    He had soot on his suit.

Pronounce the following pairs of words:

| | |
|---|---|
| [kud] | [kʊd] |
| [šud] | [šʊd] |
| [luk] | [lʊk] |
| [ful] | [fʊl] |
| [pul] | [pʊl] |

## 2. Consonant formation in general[1]

Pronounce [a - a - a - a] continuously with alternate loud and soft sections. Observe the movement of the lungs caused by the pulse of the chest or the abdominal muscles. The changes in sound are SYLLABLES; a syllable is formed by each movement of the lungs. Is there any obstruction of the stream of air which is coming from the lungs?

Pronounce the syllables [fæn fæn fæn]. Is there any obstruction of the stream of air coming from the lungs? The [f] is a partial obstruction.

Pronounce the word [kɔfi kɔfi kɔfi]. Which sounds obstruct the stream of air from the lungs? The [k] is a complete obstruction and the [f] a partial one.

Whenever a vowel occurs in a word, there is a syllable.[2] Vowels are more prominent in syllables than consonants; they are syllabic sounds. In the formation of vowel sounds there is no audible friction in the mouth. Prominence in syllables and absence of friction distinguish vowel sounds from consonant sounds.

In the production of the majority of English consonants, the stream of air from the lungs is obstructed by the organs of speech in the mouth and nose. Sometimes the air is interrupted completely; sometimes it is obstructed so that friction occurs in the mouth; sometimes it is forced over the sides of the tongue. Consonants are only obstructions of the air stream; they are less prominent in syllables than vowels; they are non-syllabic.[3]

In the following chart all the consonants of English are arranged according to the point and manner of articulation.

---

[1] Note: This is a general introductory presentation of the consonants. Mastery of the consonants and their formation is not the purpose of this lesson. Each consonant problem is presented and practiced in other lessons. This introductory section can serve as a reference in the description of individual consonants later. Do not give too much emphasis to this section in any one class period.

[2] See Lesson III, P. 33

[3] A few consonants are sometimes syllabic. These will be discussed in Lesson XIX.

## CONSONANT CHART

| Types of Consonants | | Lips | Point of Articulation | | | | |
|---|---|---|---|---|---|---|---|
| | | | Lips and Teeth | Between Teeth | Tooth Ridge | Palate | Velum |
| STOPS | vl[1] | [p] | | | [t] | | [k] |
| | vd[2] | [b] | | | [d] | | [g] |
| CONTINUANTS | | | | | | | |
| Fricatives | vl | | [f] | [Θ] | [s] | [š] | |
| | vd | | [v] | [ð] | [z] | [ž] | |
| Affricates | vl | | | | [č] | | |
| | vd | | | | [ǰ] | | |
| Nasals | vd | [m] | | | [n] | | [ŋ] |
| Glides | vd | | | | [r] | | [h] |
| | vd | | | | [y] | | [w] |
| Lateral | vd | | | | [l] | | |

### Stops and continuants

The consonants are produced by the interruption of the air stream in different man-ners. The consonants in which the air stream is completely interrupted are STOPS. The sounds in which the air stream continues to go out of the mouth or nose are CONTINU-ANTS. Vowels are all continuants, and the majority of the consonants are continuants. Which consonants are STOPS and which are CONTINUANTS?

There are several kinds of continuant consonants.

### Fricatives

The consonants in which there is audible friction in the mouth are FRICATIVES. Which consonant are FRICATIVES?

---

[1] vl = voiceless

[2] vd = voiced

Affricates

The consonants which are combinations of a stop and a fricative are AFFRICATES. Which consonants are AFFRICATES?

Nasals

The consonants in which the air stream goes out of the nose but does not go out of the mouth are NASALS. Which consonants are NASALS?

Glides

A few consonants [h], [hw], [y], [w], and [r] are formed like vowels; during the pronunciation of these consonants there is no obstruction of the air stream. These vowel-like consonants GLIDE from a consonant position to the vowel which follows them.

Lateral

In the consonant [l] the air stream comes out of the mouth over the sides of the tongue. This is a LATERAL consonant sound.

The place in the mouth where obstruction occurs during the production of a consonant is the POINT OF ARTICULATION of the consonant. Refer to the diagram of the organs of speech in III., P.30 to review the various points of articulation.

What are the points of articulation for the following sounds?

$$[b \ f \ k \ l \ m \ t \ n \ s \ ð]$$

Which of the above sounds are voiceless?

3. Flexibility of the organs of speech

In order to achieve a good English pronunciation the student needs to modify the mouth positions that he uses habitually in the pronunciation of his own language. He needs to learn to move the organs of speech consciously in many different ways. The following exercises help the student to modify the position of the organs of speech used in the production of consonants.

a) The lips assume different shapes and positions in the production of consonants. Pronounce [š]; during the sound push the lips very far forward.

b) The tongue assumes different shapes and touches many parts of the mouth in the production of consonants. Pronounce [ta] with the tip of the tongue between the teeth. Pronounce [ta] with the tip of the tongue far back in the mouth. Pronounce [ta] with the tip of the tongue in other positions in the front and the back of the mouth. Place the tip of the tongue against the tooth ridge and pronounce [l]. Do not change the position of the tongue, and pronounce the vowels [a] [e] [i] [o] [u]. The sounds should be like [l] sounds; the difference in sound is caused by the differences in the position of the back of the tongue.

### 4. Pronunciation of [t] between vowels

When the consonant [t] occurs between vowels in unstressed positions the tip of the tongue touches the tooth ridge rapidly so that a sound is produced which is different from the regular [t] sound in stressed position.[1] Notice the difference in pronunciation between the [t] sounds in TIME and CITY.

Pronounce the following.

| | | | |
|---|---|---|---|
| [létər] | [síti] | [ítıŋ] | [gɛt ıt] |
| [bétər] | [príti] | [sítıŋ] | [kət ıt] |
| [wɔ́tər] | [sítıŋ] | [lɛt ər] | [it ıt] |
| [bɔ́tər] | [ráıtıŋ] | [raıt ıt] | [et ıt] |

[hi ∫ rot ∫ ıt]                  [aı rot ə ∫ lɛtər]
[hi ∫ et ∫ ıt]                   [aı want səm ∫ wɔtər]
[hiz ∫ sıtıŋ]                    [hiz æt ðə yunıvərsıti]
[hiz ∫ raıtıŋ]                   [aım goıŋ tə ∫ gɛt ∫ ıt]
[hiz ∫ ıtıŋ]                     [aım goıŋ tə ∫ raıt ∫ ıt]

Notice the difference in pronunciation between the words WHERE and WHAT in the following sentence.[2]

Where is it?          [hwɛr ∫ ız ∫ ıt]
What is it?           [hwət ∫ ız ∫ ıt]

---

[1] Note to the teacher: This [t] sound is similar to the [r] sound in the Spanish word PERO.

[2] Note to the teacher: It should be emphasized that the sound which Spanish-speakers hear as [r] is a [t] sound in English.

Practice the following conversations.

Mr. S. [hwət ‌iz ‌ɪt]

Mr. T. [ɪts ə lɛtər]

Mr. W. [hwɛr ‌iz ‌ɪt]

Mr. X. [ɪts an ðə tebəl]

Exercise: Give an appropriate answer to the question which the teacher asks (WHERE IS IT or WHAT IS IT).

## 5. Drill on length of vowels before voiced consonants

Pronounce the following pairs of words. Notice that in the first column the vowel is followed by a voiceless consonant sound; in the second column the vowel is followed by a voiced consonant sound. Make the vowel sound longer in the second column of words than in the first.

| Long vowel | Extra-long vowel |
|:---:|:---:|
| 1 | 2 |
| [kot] | [kod] |
| [paɪp] | [paɪn] |
| [sup] | [sud] |
| [gret] | [gred] |
| [lif] | [liv] |
| [fit] | [fid] |
| [faɪt] | [faɪn] |
| [kɔt] | [kɔz] |
| [haɪt] | [haɪd] |
| [raɪt] | [raɪd] |
| [mit] | [min] |

Pronounce the following pairs of sentences.

[ši kən raɪt]            [ɪts lɔst]

[ši kən raɪd]            [ɪts lɔŋ]

6. Pronunciation of CAN and CAN'T[1]

Imitate the teacher's pronunciation of CAN in the following examples.

[aɪ kən ɡo]　　　　　　　　　[aɪ kən spik ɪŋglɪš]

[aɪ kən rɪd]　　　　　　　　　[aɪ kən spik frɛnč]

[aɪ kən raɪt]　　　　　　　　[aɪ kən rid spænɪš]

[aɪ kən stədi]　　　　　　　　[aɪ kən raɪt ɪŋglɪš]

Notice that the word CAN is pronounced [kən] in these sentences.

Pronounce the word CAN'T (negative). Be sure that the air is stopped at the end of the word. Pronounce the following sentences.

[aɪ kænt ɡo]　　　　　　　　　[aɪ kænt rid ɪŋglɪš]

[aɪ kænt rɪd]　　　　　　　　[aɪ kænt spik frɛnč]

[aɪ kænt raɪt]　　　　　　　　[aɪ kænt rid spænɪš]

[aɪ kænt stədi]　　　　　　　　[aɪ kænt raɪt ɪŋglɪš]

Notice that the word CAN'T is usually pronounced [kænt] in sentences. The word CAN (affirmative) is pronounced [kæn] with [æ] at the end of a sentence. Pronounce after the teacher:

[yɛs aɪ kæn]　　　(affirmative)

[no aɪ kænt]　　　(negative)

Notice that the [æn] in [kæn] (affirmative) is long. The [ænt] in [kænt] (negative) is short.

7. Smooth sentence rhythm

Notice the sentence rhythm in the following:

[ðɛrz ən ɪntrɪstɪŋ əsaɪnmənt ɪn ðə lɛsən]

English speakers usually do not separate syllables distinctly. The movement of the jaw is continuous with the result that English speech has smooth syllables in its sentence rhythm.

---

[1]Note to the teacher: For a fuller understanding of the problem involved here and for further discussion see the article by Eunice Pike in LANGUAGE LEARNING, Vol.II,No.2, P. 41-43.

The teacher will pronounce the sentences below with normal English pronunciation. Notice that the syllables are not separated distinctly. Many of the consonants are weak; many of the vowels are reduced, and some of them disappear. For example, [ɪz] is reduced to [z] and [hɪm] is reduced to [ɪm].

[hiz ə stuˌdənt]

[hiˈnoz ɪm]

[šiz stəˌdɪɪŋ ər vəkæbyələɛri]

The teacher will pronounce the following sentences. He will separate the syllables artificially and stress them sharply. Notice the staccato syllable.[1]

[hí - íz - ə - stu-dənt]

[hí - nóz - hím]

[ší - íz - stə́-dɪ-ɪŋ - hə́r - və-kæ-byə-lɛ-ri]

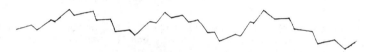

Staccato Syllables in Sentence Rhythm

Smooth Syllables in Sentence Rhythm

The preceding diagram illustrates the difference between smooth and staccato syllables.

---

[1]Note to the teacher: Spanish-speakers usually separate and stress each syllable in their pronunciation more than English speakers. The position of the jaw is held constant for a noticeable time. They use a more staccato sentence rhythm.

Compare the following two kinds of pronunciation. Observe the difference.

### Staccato Rhythm (exaggerated)

[ðɛ́r - íz - ǽn - ín-tər-ɛ́s-tíŋ - ə́-sáɪn-mə́nt - ɪn - ðə - lɛs-ən]

### Smooth Rhythm (exaggerated)

[ðɛrz n ɪntrɪstɪŋ əsaɪnmənt n ð lɛsən]

Pronounce the following phrases. Try to use a normal rapid and smooth English pronunciation. Pronounce each phrase as one word. Use the reduced form.[1]

| | | |
|---|---|---|
| [dəz i si] | [æt ɪz hom] | [ðɛrz ʃan] |
| [dəz i spik] | [æt ɪz haʊs] | [ðɛrz ʃɪm] |
| [dəz i baɪ] | [æt ɪz klæs] | [ðɛrz ʃemz] |
| [dəz i kəm] | [æt ɪz dɛsk] | [ðɛrz ʃɔrʃ] |
| [dəz i it] | [æt ɪz rʊm] | |
| [dəz i sɪŋ] | [æt ɪz stɔr] | |
| [dəz i tič] | [æt ɪz strɪt] | |
| [dəz i wərk] | [æt ɪz bæŋk] | |

[ðə mæn ɪz kəmɪŋ ət wən]
[ðə mæn ɪz kəmɪŋ ət tu]
[ðə mæn ɪz kəmɪŋ ət Θri]
[ðə mæn ɪz kəmɪŋ ət fɔr]

---

[1] Note to the teacher: In order to learn smooth English rhythm, Spanish-speakers need to use reduced forms whenever reduced forms are used by English speakers.

## PRONUNCIATION

1. Review of [ɪ], [ɛ], [æ]
2. Pronunciation of [Θ] and [ð]
3. Pronunciation of [t] and [d]
4. Pronunciation of [d] contrasted with [ð]
5. Pronunciation of [t] contrasted with [Θ]
6. Pronunciation of WITH and WITHOUT

Review

a) What are the points of articulation for the following sounds?

[d l b k r š n Θ ŋ]

b) Practice the following conversations from memory.

      Mr. S.  What is it?

      Mr. T.  It's a letter.

      Mr. W.  Where is it?

      Mr. X.  It's on the table.

c) Pronounce the following sentences.

1. I can read English.
2. They can understand the teacher.
3. The students can go to class.
4. We can attend the lecture.
5. She can study at the library.
6. Mary can write letters in the afternoon.
7. He can eat many kinds of food.
8. Mr. Wilson can go by train.
9. They can walk very fast.
10. John can go to the movies.

d) Change the sentences in section (c) to the negative.

Example: I can't read English.

e) Repeat rapidly the following sentences with a uniform rythm.

[ar yə ˈraɪtɪŋ ðə ˈnəmbər]

[ar yə ˈraɪtɪŋ ðə nəmbər əv ðə ˈrum]

[ar yə ˈraɪtɪŋ ðə nəmbər əv ðə larj ˈrum]

[ar yə ˈraɪtɪŋ ðə nəmbər əv ðə vɛri larj ˈrum]

## 1. Review of [ɪ], [ɛ], [æ]

Pronounce the following contrasts:

| | | |
|---|---|---|
| [pɪn] | [pɛn] | [pæn] |
| [bítər] | [bétər] | [bǽtər] |
| [bɪt] | [bɛt] | [bæt] |
| [tɪn] | [tɛn] | [tæn] |
| [trɪk] | [trɛk] | [træk] |

Pronounce the following:

| | |
|---|---|
| [ɪt wəz ə bɪt] | [aɪ si ðə pɪn] |
| [ɪt wəz ə bɛt] | [aɪ si ðə pɛn] |
| [ɪt wəz ə bæt] | [aɪ si ðə pæn] |

## 2. Pronunciation of [Θ] and [ð]

The consonant [ð] is a VOICED FRICATIVE. In the pronunciation of [ð] the tip of the tongue is between the teeth. The consonant [Θ] is a VOICELESS FRICATIVE. In the pronunciation of [Θ] the tip of the tongue is between the teeth.

Notice the tongue position for [Θ] and [ð] in the diagram. The main difference between these sounds is that [Θ] is voiceless and [ð] is voiced.

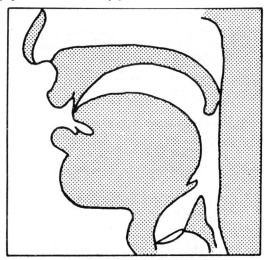

Tongue position of [Θ] and [ð]

Place the tip of the tongue between the teeth and blow air through the mouth. The teacher will pronounce the sound [Θ]. Retain the position of the tongue and mimic his pronunciation. Move the tongue forward and backward until you can mimic the teacher exactly.

The teacher will pronounce the following words: [Θɪŋk] [Θɪŋ] [Θæŋk]. Mimic his pronunciation; retain the tip of the tongue between the teeth during the first sound of the words; blow air through the mouth during the first sound.

The teacher will pronounce the following words: [ðæt], [ðoz], [ðɪs]. Mimic his pronunciation. Retain the tip of the tongue between the teeth during the first sound of the words; blow air through the mouth during the first sound. Move the tongue slightly forward or backward until you can mimic the teacher exactly.

Pronounce the following.

| [Θɪŋ] | [Θɪn] | [ðɪs] | [ðɛr] |
| [Θɪŋk] | [tiΘ] | [ðæt] | [brəðər] |
| [Θɔt] | [dɛΘ] | [ðe] | [fáðər] |
| [Θæŋk] | [Θíətər] | [ðɛn] | [áðər] |

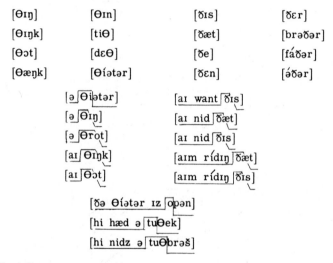

Practice the following conversations.

John.          [hwɛr ɪz ɪz brəðər]

Richard.       [hɪz brəðərz ɪn vɛnəzwelə]

Richard.       [du yə want ðə Θíətər tɪkɪt]

John.          [yɛs Θæŋk yu]

3. Pronunciation of [t] and [d]

The consonant [d] is a VOICED STOP. In the pronunciation of [d] the tip of the tongue is against the tooth ridge. The consonant [t] is a VOICELESS STOP.

Notice the tongue position for [t] and [d] in the diagram. The only difference between these sounds is that [t] is voiceless and [d] is voiced.

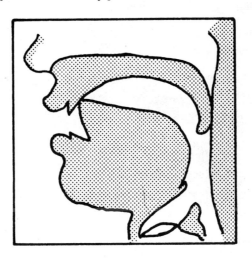

Tongue position for [t] and [d]

Pronounce the sound [t] in the following words with aspiration. Be sure that your tongue does not touch the teeth.[1]

| | | |
|---|---|---|
| [tébəl] | [tɛl] | [əténd] |
| [tǽksi] | [ti] | [tíkɪt] |
| [test] | [tost] | [témprəčər] |
| [tɔk] | [téləfon] | [téləgræm] |

---

[1]Note to the teacher: Spanish speaking people pronounce [t] with the tongue against the teeth. When the tongue touches the teeth the consonant produced sounds like [Ө] to English-speaking people. Compare the pronunciation of [t] in Spanish TOMAS and English THOMAS.

Pronounce the following words. Be sure the tip of the tongue does not touch the teeth when you pronounce [d].

| | | |
|---|---|---|
| [det] | [dáktər] | [díšɪz] |
| [dɛsk] | [du] | [dɪstrɔ́ɪ] |
| [déntɪst] | [dəz] | [drɪŋk] |
| [de] | [dɔ́tər] | [dɪsáɪd] |

Pronounce the following sentences.

[hi hæz tu nu ʃtaɪz]                    [hiz ə daktər]

[pliz tɛl mi ðə ʃtaɪm]                   [hiz ə dɛntɪst]

[wɪr goɪŋ tə hæv ə ʃtɛst]                [aɪ hæv ə ʃdallər]

[mek ə ʃti]

[dont təč yər ʃtiθ]

[dont təč yər ʃtiθ hwɛn yə mek ə ʃti]

[dont təč yər ʃtiθ hwɛn yə mek ə ʃdi]

Practice the following conversations.

Engineer A.  [hwət ʃɪz i]

Engineer B.  [hiz ə ʃdaktər]

Teacher A.  [kən yə ʃtɛl mi ðə ʃtaɪm]

Teacher B.  [ɪts ʃtɛn tə ʃtu]

4. Pronunciation of [d] contrasted with [ð][1]

Pronounce [de] DAY and [ðe] THEY. Notice that English [d] is a STOP sound and [ð] is a FRICATIVE sound.

---

[1] Note to the teacher: Spanish-speakers sometimes pronounce [d] as a stop and sometimes as a fricative. Notice the difference in the [d] in Spanish DEDO and English DADDY.

Pronounce the following words.

|  1 [d]  |  2 [ð]  |
|---------|---------|
| [de]    | [ðe]    |
| [do]    | [ðo]    |
| [dɛn]   | [ðɛn]   |
| [daɪ]   | [ðaɪ]   |
| [dɛr]   | [ðɛr]   |
| [doz]   | [ðoz]   |
| [lod]   | [loð]   |
| [sid]   | [sið]   |

Pronounce the following sounds rapidly in succession. Notice the difference in tongue position for the sounds [ð] and [d].

[ðə - də - ðə - də - ðə - də - ðə - də]

| [ðə dɛntɪst] | [ðə det]    | [ðə fud]    |
| [ðə dɛsk]    | [ðə de]     | [ɪz gʊd]    |
| [ðə daktər]  | [ðə dɪfrəns]| [yɛstərdi]  |

Practice the following conversation using different days of the week.

Student A.  [hwət de ɪz təde]
Student B.  [təde ɪz _____ ]

Practice the following sentences. Be sure to pronounce [d] with the front of the tongue touching the tooth ridge.

[ɪz ðə fud gʊd]              [yɛs ɪts gʊd]
[wəz ɪt gʊd yɛstərdi]        [yɛs ɪt wəz gʊd]

Memorize the following conversation. Pay particular attention to the sounds [t], [d], [ɵ], and [ð].[1]

---

[1] This is a particularly difficult conversation and should be used with caution so that students do not become discouraged. It can be simplified by using only the first and the last lines.

John.    [ar yə goɪŋ tə ðə|dæns]

Thomas. [hwəts ðə|det]

John.    [ɪts an ðə twɛnti|Θərd]

Thomas. [yɛ̀s aɪ|Θɪŋk|aɪm goɪŋ tə|go]

## 5. Pronunciation of [t] contrasted with [Θ]

Pronounce the following words. In the pronunciation of [t] the front of the tongue touch-es the tooth ridge, IT DOES NOT TOUCH THE TEETH. In the pronunciation of [Θ] the tongue is between the teeth.

|       1 [t] |       2 [Θ] |
|-------------|-------------|
| [tɪn]       | [Θɪn]       |
| [tæŋk]      | [Θæŋk]      |
| [taɪ]       | [Θaɪ]       |
| [tɔt]       | [Θɔt]       |
| [tim]       | [Θim]       |
| [tri]       | [Θri]       |
| [dɛt]       | [dɛΘ]       |
| [pæt]       | [pæΘ]       |

Pronounce the following verse:    (Note expecially the length of the accented syllables)

[ðə tičər|tɔ́t|ən|tɔ́t|ən|tɔ́t

bət no wən|nú|ðə|Θɔts|ši|Θɔt]

## 6. Pronunciation of WITH and WITHOUT

Pronounce the following phrases.

[wɪð maɪ|faðər]              [wɪðaut maɪ|faðər]

[wɪð maɪ|frɛnd]             [wɪðaut maɪ|frɛnd]

[wɪð maɪ|brəðər]           [wɪðaut maɪ|brəðər]

[wɪð maɪ|sɪstər]            [wɪðaut maɪ|sɪstər]

[wɪð maɪ|tičər]             [wɪðaut maɪ|tičər]

Complete the following sentences with phrases from above.

[hiz góɪŋ_____]

[ar yə góɪŋ_____]

## PRONUNCIATION

1. Review of front vowels
2. Pronunciation of [s] and [z]
3. Consonant combinations with [s]
4. Pronunciation of [s] contrasted with [Ө]
5. 3-2 intonation curve
6. Exercise on suppression of stress

Review

a) Pronounce the following words.

[taɪ]                [daɪ]                [Өaɪ]                [ðaɪ]

b) Review the following conversations from memory.

Richard.  Do you want the theater ticket?
John.     Yes, thank you.

Doctor A. Can you tell me the time?
Doctor B. It's ten to two

John.     Are you going to the dance?
Thomas.   What's the date?
John.     It's on the twenty-third.
Thomas.   Yes. I think I'm going to go.

1. Review of front vowels

Repeat each of the front vowels three times.

[i i i    ɪ ɪ ɪ    e e e    ɛ ɛ ɛ    æ æ æ]

Pronounce the following contrasts:

[bit]        [bɪt]        [bet]        [bɛt]        [bæt]

[sit]        [sɪt]        [set]        [sɛt]        [sæt]

[mit]        [mɪt]        [met]        [mɛt]        [mæt]

Pronounce the following sentences in rapid alternation.

1. [aɪ mɛt ɪm]    I met him. (yesterday)

2. [aɪ mit ɪm]    I meet him. (every day)

Pronounce the following:

[ðə pæn]        [ðə pɛn]        [ðə pɪn]        [ðə pen]

2. Pronunciation of [s] and [z]

The consonant [s] is a VOICELESS FRICATIVE. In the pronunciation of [s] the sides of the tongue are against the tooth ridge. The front of the tongue forms a small groove in order to focus the air stream against the tooth ridge and the upper teeth. The consonant [z] is a VOICED FRICATIVE. The position of the tongue is the same as in [s].

Notice the tongue position and shape of the tongue for the sounds [s] and [z].[1] The only difference between these sounds is that [s] is voiceless and [z] is voiced.

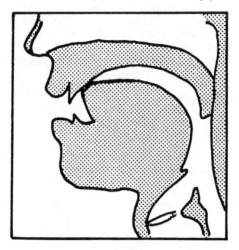

Tongue position for [s] and [z]

Pronounce the following sounds.

[sss   zzz   sss   zzz   sss   zzz]

[sssi   zzzi   sssi   zzzi]

[aɪs   aɪz   aɪs   aɪz   aɪs   aɪz][2]

Pronounce the following words.

|   1 [s]   |   2 [z]   |
|-----------|-----------|
| [si]      | [zi]      |
| [su]      | [zu]      |
| [sil]     | [zil]     |
| [sɪp]     | [zɪp]     |

---

[1] Note to the teacher: Spanish [s] is generally pronounced with the tongue farther forward than the tongue position of English [s], and the tip of the tongue is turned slightly upward. English speakers think that they hear [Θ] when the tongue is pushed too far forward and the tip of the tongue is turned upward.

[2] At the end of a word the [z] sound is pronounced rather softly. It is better to emphasize the vowel preceding the [z] sound than to pronounce it with a strong buzzing sound. (See Lesson XI. P.92)

|          |          |
|----------|----------|
| [aɪs]    | [aɪz]    |
| [lus]    | [luz]    |
| [res]    | [rez]    |
| [ǰus]    | [ǰuz]    |
| [hɪs]    | [hɪz]    |
| [lési]   | [lési]   |

Pronounce the following sentences.

[pliz sɪŋ ə sɔ́ŋ]

[ðə kanʦərt ɪz ət sɛ́vən]

[kən yə ǽnsər ɪz kwɛ́sʧən]

[pliz pæs ðə sɪgərɛ́ts]

[səm əv ðə stúdənts ər sɪ́rɪəs]

[səm əv əs wɛnt tə ðə sɪ́ti]

[ðə bɔɪ sɛldəm stə́diz]

[hi noz mɛni sɔ́ŋz]

[ðə kanʦərt wəzənt ɛkspɛ́nsɪv]

## 3. Consonant combinations with [s]

Pronounce the following syllables.[1] The symbol [:] indicates that the sound is long.

[s : : : : pa]    [s : : : : ta]    [s : : : : ka]

[s : : : tra]    [s : : : kra]    [s : : : pra]    [s : : : kwa]

Pronounce the following syllables. Be sure that you pronounce [s] and not [z] in these combinations.

[s : : : : wa]    [s : : : : ma]    [s : : : : na]    [s : : : : la]

Pronounce the following words. Observe especially the initial combinations.

| [stæmp]  | [stap]    | [stə́di]  | [stænd]  |
|----------|-----------|----------|----------|
| [spɪč]   | [spǽnɪš]  | [spik]   | [spɛ́šəl] |
| [sket]   | [skarf]   | [skul]   | [skaɪ]   |
| [slip]   | [slo]     | [slaɪd]  | [smɛl]   |
| [sno]    | [smok]    | [smaɪl]  | [sprɪŋ]  |
| [skwɛr]  | [skrim]   | [strit]  | [swɪm]   |

---

[1] Note to the teacher: This exercise is intended to combat the tendency of Spanish speakers to pronounce an initial vowel before [s]. For review of clusters [pra] and [kra] see p.59

Practice the following sentences.

[du yə laɪk tə ˺skeˌt]

[du yə laɪk tə ˺swɪm]

[du yə laɪk tə ˺slip]

[hɪ laɪks tə ˺smok]

[mɪs grin ɪz əˌslip]

Pronounce the following pair of sentences.

He's sleeping        [hiz ˺sliˌpɪŋ]

He's leaping         [hiz ˺liˌpɪŋ]

Practice the following conversation.

Student.   [hu ɪz ˺goɪŋ tə ðə ˺kanˌsərt]

Teacher.   [səm əv ðə ˺studənts]

Student.   [hwɛn dəz ðə kansərt bɪˌgɪn]

Teacher.   [ət sɛvən əˌklak]

Student.   [kən yə ˺smok ˺ət ðə kansərt]

Teacher.   [smoˌkɪŋ ɪz nat pərˌmɪˌtɪd]

## 4. Pronunciation of [s] contrasted with [Θ]

The tongue position is different in the pronunciation of [s] and [Θ]. In the pronunciation of [Θ] the tongue is placed between the teeth. When you pronounce [s] keep your teeth closed.

Pronounce the following words and sentences.

|   1 [s]   |   2 [Θ]   |
|-----------|-----------|
| [sɪŋ]     | [Θɪŋ]     |
| [sɪŋk]    | [Θɪŋk]    |
| [sæŋk]    | [Θæŋk]    |
| [saɪ]     | [Θaɪ]     |
| [sim]     | [Θim]     |
| [pæs]     | [pæΘ]     |
| [mɪs]     | [mɪΘ]     |
| [sɪ́knəs]  | [Θɪ́knəs]  |

[Θæŋk yʊ fər ðə sɪgərɛts]

[aɪ Θɪŋk hiz hɪr]

[ðɛr ər mɛni ɪntrɪstɪŋ Θɪŋz ɪn ðə sɪti]

Pronounce the following pair of sentences.

Mr. Smith likes to think [θɪŋk].

Mr. Smith likes to sing [sɪŋ].

Memorize the following conversations.

Lawyer S.  [hwət ər yə θɪŋkɪŋ əbaut]

Doctor A.  [aɪm θɪŋkɪŋ əbaut maɪ prənənsɪešən]

Dentist R.  [hwɛr dəz mɪstər smɪθ lɪv]

Professor T.  [hi lɪvz an sauθ dɪvɪžən]

## 5. 3-2 intonation curve

The 3-2 intonation is frequently used to indicate something which is incomplete. It is often used in a series of words or phrases. This intonation is frequently used in counting.[1]

Pronounce the following words.

wən    tu    θri    fɔr    faɪv    sɪks    sɛvən    et    naɪn    tɛn    ɪlɛvən

twɛlv    θərtin    fɔrtin    fɪftin    (twɛntɪ    wən    twɛntɪ    tu    twɛntɪ    θri

twɛntɪ    fɔr)

The 3-2 intonation is sometimes used to indicate a series of things or actions. Pronounce the following.

[mɛn wɪmɪn ənd čɪldrən]

[brɛkfəst lənč ən dɪnər]

[hi stud əp tərnd ənd wɛnt aut]

[hi ridz raɪts ən spiks ɪngliš]

Pronounce the following. Use the 3-2 intonation curve as marked.

[aɪ hæftə baɪ ə pɛnsəl ə pɛn ən səm pepər]

[maɪ faðər maɪ məðər ən maɪ brəðər ər kəmɪŋ]

[wi hæv brɛkfəst lənč ən dɪnər ət ðə haus]

[hɛlən jan ən jɪm ər goɪŋ wɪð əs]

[wi dɪdənt hæv ɛni šugər kɔfi ər bətər]

---

[1] Note to the teacher: In rapid counting a 2-3 intonation curve is used. In very slow or forceful counting the 2-4 intonation curve is usually used. Spanish-speakers usually pronounce this intonation curve with a pitch that is too high. Frequently they use a 2-1 intonation curve. The prominence of this high pitch among Spanish-speakers is the reason that the introduction of the medial 3-2 intonation curve into the lessons has been delayed. In order to combat the tendency to use too high a pitch, students should be drilled intensively on intonation curves which cause the pitch to fall. They should be drilled also on sentences with only one intonation curve in order to combat the tendency to use a 3-2 curve on each word. This tendency is especially prominent in reading style.

The 3-2 intonation curve can be used in questions which begin with some form of BE or DO.[1] Questions spoken with a 3-2 intonation curve are slightly more formal than the same questions spoken with 2-4 intonation curve. If the 3-2 intonation curve is used too much it results in a feeling of insincerity and artificiality on the part of the hearer.

Pronounce the following sentences.

[ɪz i ə tičər]                 [ɪz ðə mæn hɪr]

[dəz i laɪk mɪlk]          [du yə laɪk muvɪz]

[ɪz ɪt kold]                  [wəz ši ə nərs]

[ar ðe student̄s]          [du yə əndərstǽnd]

[ɪz ši ərli]                 [dəz ɪt ɛksplen ðəm]

[ar wi impruvɪŋ]        [du ðe æsk kwɛsčənz]

## 6. Exercise on suppression of stress

The teacher will read the following sentences. Notice the difference in the number of stresses.

[ðə prəfɛsər ɪz ən ɪntɛlɪjənt mæn]

[ðə prəfɛsərz ən ɪntɛlɪjənt mæn]

In rapid speech stresses are often suppressed or omitted in order to maintain smooth sentence rhythm. Stress is often retained only on words that need special emphasis.

The teacher will read the following two groups of sentences. Observe the stress of slow speech in the first group. Observe the suppression of stress in the rapid pronunciation of the second group.

| Slow speech | Rapid speech |
|---|---|
| [ðə čaɪld ɪz ə prɪti gərl] | [ðə čaɪldz ə prɪti gərl] |
| [hi ɪz rɪdɪŋ ə larǰ bʊk] | [hiz rɪdɪŋ ə larǰ bʊk] |
| [ðə daktər kəmz tə ðə haʊs] | [ðə daktər kəmz tə ðə haʊs] |
| [hwɛn ɪz ðə daktər kəmɪŋ] | [hwɛnz ðə daktər kəmɪŋ] |

Pronounce one sentence from each of the above groups.

---

[1] Note to the teacher: Questions that have the grammatical form of statements often have the 3-2 intonation curve.

[hɪz ə student]

[hɪz kəmɪŋ]

Spanish speakers have a tendency to use this form and this intonation, and they need practice on the common question form with reversed work order. (See Grammar Lesson I.)

## PRONUNCIATION

1. Review of [æ] and [ə]
2. Pronunciation of [š] and [ž]
3. Pronunciation of [š] contrasted with [č]
4. Pronunciation of [ǰ]
5. Contrast of [š], [č], and [ǰ]
6. Rhythm drills
7. Pronunciation of IT'S and THERE'S

### Review

a) Pronounce the following words.

[su]     [zu]     [aɪs]     [aɪz]     [lesi]     [lezi]

b) Practice the following conversations from memory.

| | |
|---|---|
| Student: | Who is going to the concert? |
| Teacher: | Some of the students. |
| Student: | When does the concert begin? |
| Teacher: | At seven o'clock. |
| Student: | Can you smoke at the concert? |
| Teacher: | Smoking is not permitted. |
| Lawyer S. | What are you thinking about? |
| Doctor A. | I'm thinking about my pronunciation. |

### 1. Review of [æ] and [ə]

Pronounce the following contrasting pairs of words:

| [bæt] | [bət] | | [kæt] | [kət] |
|---|---|---|---|---|
| [fæn] | [fən] | | [kæp] | [kəp] |
| [tæn] | [tən] | | [sæm] | [səm] |

Practice the following paragraph:

[əŋkəl hɛnri wəz həŋgri.     ðɛr wəz nəθiŋ in ðə haʊs fər ə həŋgri mæn tə it.

Uncle Henry was hungry.     There was nothing in the house for a hungry man to eat.

əŋkəl hɛnri wəz æŋgri.     pʊr həŋgri æŋgri əŋkəl hɛnri]

Uncle Henry was angry.     Poor hungry, angry Uncle Henry.

### 2. Pronunciation of [š] and [ž]

The consonant sound [š] is a VOICELESS FRICATIVE. During the pronunciation of [š] the tip of the tongue is very close to the tooth ridge and the middle of the tongue is close to the palate; the tongue is grooved and the lips are pushed outward. The teeth are close together. The sound [ž] is a VOICED FRICATIVE.

Notice the position of the tongue and lips during the pronunciation of [š] and [ž]. The only difference between these sounds is that [š] is voiceless and [ž] is voiced.

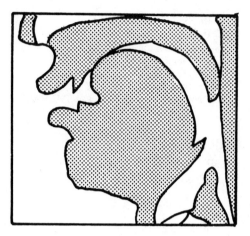

Lip and tongue position for [š] and [ž]

Pronounce the following words and sentences.

| | | | |
|---|---|---|---|
| [šep] | [brəš] | [wɔ́šɪz] | [kæšɪ́r] |
| [šev] | [wɔš] | [díšɪz] | [ɪnvɪtéšən] |
| [šuz] | [kæš] | [kǽšɪz] | [ɛgzæ̀mɪnešən] |
| | | | |
| [vížən] | [ruž] | [kənklúžən] | [dɪvížən] |
| [mɛ́žər] | [gəráž] | [prəvížən] | [kənfyúžən] |

[ðɛr ševɪŋ]

[hɪz ə kæšɪr]

[šɪz wɔšɪŋ ðə díšɪz]

[šɪz wɔšɪŋ ər hɛr]

[ðə dɪsɪžən ɪz faɪnəl]

[hɪz vɪžən ɪz gʊd]

[ðə kənklužən wəz ɪntrɪstɪŋ]

[ðə ɛgzæmɪnešən wəz izi]

## 3. Pronunciation of [š] contrasted with [č]

The consonant sound [č] is a voiceless affricate.[1] The lips, tongue, and teeth are in almost the same position as for [š]. However, in the pronunciation of [č] the tip of the tongue touches the tooth ridge during the first part of the sound.

Notice the difference in pronunciation in SHEEP [šip] and CHEAP [čip].

---

[1] See XI. P. 89, 90

Pronounce the following words.

| 1 [š] | 2 [č] |
|-------|-------|
| [šu]  | [ču]  |
| [šip] | [čip] |
| [šɪn] | [čɪn] |
| [šuz] | [čuz] |
| [šɪp] | [čɪp] |
| [šɪr] | [čɪr] |

Pronounce the following words.

| [čaɪld] | [šɛr] | [tíčər] | [wač] | [kæš] |
| [čɪn] | [šu] | [témprəčər] | [tič] | [brəš] |
| [čɛr] | [šek] | [lékčər] | [lənč] | [wɔš] |
| [čik] | [šaɪ] | [fə́rnɪčər] | [məč] | [klæš] |

Practice the following pairs of sentences.

He hurt his shin [šɪn].
He hurt his chin [čɪn].

Practice the following sentences.

[ðə čaɪld hæz nu šuz]

[hiz goɪŋ tə kæš ə čɛk]

[ši med ə šɔrt spič]

[hiz goɪŋ tə šev]

[hiz goɪŋ tə tek ə šauər]

[ðə tičər ɪz itɪŋ lənč]

[aɪ laɪk pəteto čɪps vɛri məč]

[ðə témprəčər ɪz vɛri haɪ]

Memorize the following conversation.

Student C.  [ar wɪ goɪŋ tə hæv ən ɛgzæmɪnešən]

Student D.  [yɛs bət ðə tičər sɛz its goɪŋ tə bi šɔrt]

4. Pronunciation of [ǰ]

The consonant sound [ǰ] is a VOICED AFFRICATE.[1] The lips, tongue, and teeth are in almost the same position as for [ž]. However, in the pronunciation of [ǰ] the tip of the tongue touches the tooth ridge and stops the air stream during the first part of the sound.

| [ǰok] | [ǰɔrǰ] | [sə́bǰɪkt] | [eǰ] |
| [ǰəst] | [ǰemz] | [mǽnɪǰər] | [pǽkɪǰ] |
| [ǰun] | [ǰan] | [rɪlɪǰən] | [mérɪǰ] |

---

[1]See XI. P.89,90

[ǰɪm̩ wantɪd ə ǰ́ab]

[ðə rod ɪz vɛri denǰərəs]

[wi ɛnǰoɪd ðə ǰ́ok]

[hiz ə gʊd mænɪǰər]

[šiz goɪŋ tə kələmbɪə ɪn ǰun]

[ǰorǰ ɪz ə ǰɛntəlmən]

## 5. Contrast of [š], [č], and [ǰ][1]

Pronounce the following words.

| 1 [š] | 2 [č] | 3 [ǰ] |
|---|---|---|
| [šu] | [ču] | [ǰu] |
| [šɪn] | [čɪn] | [ǰɪn] |
| [šip] | [čip] | [ǰip] |
| [šuz] | [čuz] | [ǰuz] |

Practice the following sentences.

[ðə šuz ar vɛri larǰ]

[hɛlən ɪz wɔšɪŋ ðə dɪšɪz]

[ðə pækɪǰ ɪz vɛri ɪmportənt]

[ðə čaɪld kət ɪz čik]

[ðə spič wəz šɔrt]

[hɪz šoldər ɪz blidɪŋ]

[ðə ɛksplənešən wəz ɪntrɪstɪŋ]

Memorize the following conversations.

Clerk.     [hwɪč šuz du yə prɪfər]

Student.     [aɪ laɪk ðiz šuz vɛri məč]

Lawyer S.     [hwɛr dəz ǰan wərk]

Lawyer T.     [hi hæz ə ǰab ɪn ðə laɪbrɛri]

## 6. Rhythm drills

Read the following series of sentences with smooth sentence rhythm. The teacher will indicate the speed of pronunciation by tapping with a pencil. Pronounce the sentences so that the interval between the stresses does not change.

---

[1] Note to the teacher. The sound [ž] has been omitted from this section because it is not used with great frequency in English. It never appears in initial position in English words and sometimes is replaced by [ǰ] in final position as in GARAGE.

[ðə ˥mɛn˩ ɪn ar klæs ˥smȯk]

[ðə yəŋ ˥mɛn˩ ɪn ar klæs ˥smȯk]

[ðə yəŋ ˥mɛn˩ ɪn ar ɪŋglɪš klæs ˥smȯk]

[ðɪ əðər yəŋ ˥mɛn˩ ɪn ar ɪŋglɪš klæs ˥smȯk]

[ðɪ əðər yəŋ ˥mɛn˩ ɪn ar ɪŋglɪš klæs dont ˥smȯk]

[ðə ˥boɪz˩ ɪn ar klæs ˥stədi]

[ðɪ ɪntɛlɪjənt ˥boɪz˩ ɪn ar klæs ˥stədi]

[ðɪ ɪntɛlɪjənt ˥boɪz˩ ɪn ar pronənsiešən klæs ˥stədi]

[ðɪ ɪntɛlɪjənt ˥boɪz˩ ɪn ar pronənsiešən klæs dont ˥stədi]

[ðɪ əðər ɪntɛlɪjənt ˥boɪz˩ ɪn ar pronənsiešən klæs dont ˥stədi][1]

7. Pronunciation of IT'S and THERE'S

Pronounce the following sentences.

[ɪts ə naɪs ˥de]

[ðɛrz ə gud ˥muvi ət ðə stet ˥θiətər]

Be sure that you pronounce the final [s] and [z] in the reduced forms [ɪts] and [ðɛrz] in the following exercise.

| | |
|---|---|
| [ɪts ə gud ˥kansərt] | [ðɛrz ə ˥buk an ðə ˥tebəl] |
| [ɪts ə bɪg ˥dɔg] | [ðɛrz ə ˥mæn ɪn ðə ˥bæŋk] |
| [ɪts ə larj ˥tebəl] | [ðɛrz ə ˥dɔg ɪn ðə ˥stɔr] |
| [ɪts ən old ˥tæksi] | [ðɛrz ə ˥wumən ɪn ðə ˥kar] |
| [ɪts ə bɪg ˥blækbɔrd] | [ðɛrz ə ˥bɔɪ an ðə ˥kɔrnər] |
| [ɪts ə gud ˥čɛr] | [ðɛrz ə ˥pɛn an ðə ˥dɛsk] |
| [ɪts ən ɪntrɪstɪŋ ˥muvi] | [ðɛrz ə ˥tičər ɪn ðə ˥laɪbrɛri] |
| [ɪts ə dɪfɪkəlt ˥klæs] | [ðɛrz ə ˥daktər ɪn ðə ˥klæs] |

---

[1]Note to the teacher: Additional rhythm drills may be practiced when needed by merely substituting in the above exercises the following: STUDENTS, or GIRLS for BOYS; SCHOOL for CLASS; PRACTICE, or LISTEN for STUDY.

## PRONUNCIATION

1. Review of back vowels
2. Pronunciation of [f] and [v]
3. Pronunciation of [b] contrasted with [v]
4. Rhythm drills with 3 stresses

Review

a) Pronounce the following pair of sentences.

He hurt his shin.
He hurt his chin.

b) Pronounce the following words.

| [šuz] | [čuz] | [ǰuz] |
|-------|-------|-------|
| [šip] | [čip] | [ǰip] |

c) Practice the following conversations from memory.

Clerk.      Which shoes do you prefer?
Student.    I like these shoes very much.

Lawyer S.   Where does John work?
Lawyer T.   He has a job in the library.

d) Pronounce the following sentences with smooth sentence rhythm.

1. The men in our class smoke.
2. The young men in our class smoke.
3. The young men in our English class smoke.
4. The other young men in our English class smoke.
5. The other young men in our English class don't smoke.

e) Pronounce the following sentences. Be sure to pronounce IT'S and THERE'S with reduced forms.

1. It's a beautiful day.
2. There's a man in the store.
3. It's an excellent example.
4. It's a good book.
5. There's a concert tonight.
6. There's an interesting letter on my desk.
7. It's a difficult class.
8. It's an expensive automobile.

1. Review of back vowels

Repeat each of the back vowels three times.

[uuu    uuu    ooo    ɔɔɔ]

Pronounce the following contrasts:

| | | | |
|---|---|---|---|
| [luk] | [lʊk] | [lon] | [lɔn] |
| [pul] | [pʊl] | [pol] | [pɔl] |
| [but] | [bʊk] | [bot] | [bɔt] |

Pronounce the following sentences in rapid alternation.

1. [aɪ sɛd ˈluk]     I said, "Luke."

2. [aɪ sɛd ˈlʊk]     I said, "look."

1. [aɪ sɛd ˈbot]     I said, "boat."

2. [aɪ sɛd ˈbɔt]     I said, "bought."

## 2. Pronunciation of [f] and [v]

The consonant [v] is a VOICED FRICATIVE. In the pronunciation of [v] the lower lip is against the upper teeth. The consonant [f] is a VOICELESS FRICATIVE that is, air continues to pass between the lower teeth and upper lip. In the pronunciation of [f] the lower lip is against the upper teeth.

Notice the position of the lips for [f] and [v] in the diagram. The only difference between these sounds is that [f] is voiceless and [v] is voiced.

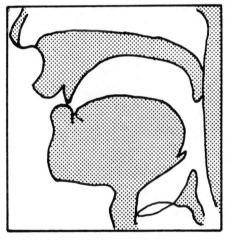

Tongue position for [f] and [v]

Pronounce the following words.[1]

---

[1] Note to the teacher: Students should be reminded that both of these sounds should be pronounced with the lips in the same position. Spanish-speakers have a tendency to pronounce [v] with lips completely closed so that the sound is confused with English [b].

1 [f]          2 [v]

[fæn]          [væn]

[faɪ]          [vaɪ]

[faɪn]         [vaɪn]

[fæt]          [væt]

[fɔn]          [vɔn]

[fil]          [vil]

[lif]          [liv]

[bəlif]        [bəliv]

[fɔr]              [farm]            [æftərnún]

[fɛr]              [fæst]            [kæfətíryə]

[fɔl]              [fæt]             [téləfon]

[fərst]            [faɪnd]           [əfékt]

[véri]             [ǽvənyu]          [rɪsív]

[vízɪt]            [lívɪŋ]           [ædváɪs]

[hévi]             [gívɪŋ]           [prəváɪd]

[lívɪŋ]            [šévɪŋ]           [kənvíns]

[ə lat əv ǽpəlz]

[ə lat əv íŋk]

[ə lat əv ɛgzæmɪnéšənz]

[ə lat əv ɛgzǽmpəlz]

Memorize the following conversation.

Engineer A.   [ar yə goɪŋ tə vízɪt ðə fɔrd fǽktri]

Engineer B.   [yɛ́s wɪr goɪŋ ðɪs æftərnún]

Engineer A.   [hau far ɪz ɪt tə ðə fǽktri]

Engineer B.   [ɪts ɔlmost fɔrti máɪlz]

3. Pronunciation of [b] contrasted with [v]

The consonant [b] is a VOICED STOP. In the pronunciation of [b] the lips are completely closed. Notice the position of the lips in the diagram.

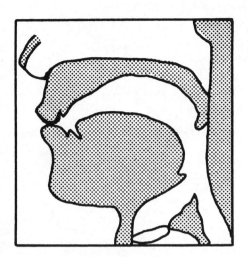

Tongue position for [b]

Pronounce the following words. Be sure that your lips are completely closed when you pronounce the [b] sound.

[wi bɪgɪn]                              [ðə batəl]

[wi bɪkəm]                             [ðə blækbɔrd]

[wi dɪskraɪb]                          [hi brɔt]

[ə jab]                                [hi brok]

Pronounce the following words.

| 1 [b] | 2 [v] |
|-------|-------|
| [bæt] | [væt] |
| [ben] | [ven] |
| [bɛri] | [vɛri] |
| [bæn] | [væn] |
| [bot] | [vot] |
| [rob] | [rov] |

Pronounce the following sentences.

[aɪ laɪk muvɪz vɛri məč]

[aɪ lɪv ɪn æn arbər]

[hiz pleɪŋ vali bɔl]

[ðæts gʊd ædvaɪs]

[aɪ laɪk bɛriz]

Memorize the following conversations.

Professor A.  [hwɛr du yə ˈlɪv]

Professor B.  [aɪ lɪv ɪn æn ˈarbər]

Student C.   [wəz ðə muvi ˈgʊd]

Student D.   [noʊ ɪt wəz vɛri ˈbæd]

## 4. Rhythm drills with 3 stresses[1]

Practice the following conversation with a normal rapid smooth pronunciation. Use the 2-3 2-3 2-4 intonation.

Mr. S.  [pardən mi bət yu ar ˈitɪŋ maɪ ˈsæləd]

Mr. J.  [ænd ˈyu ar ˈitɪŋ maɪ ˈbrɛd]

Mr. S.  [wetər pliz brɪŋ əs səm mor ˈsæləd n ənəðər pis əv ˈbrɛd]

Note the places of potential stress (----) in the following sentence:

[ǰan ˌwəz ˈstədiɪŋ ɪn ɪz ˈrum ˈlæst ˈnaɪt]

Practice the following questions and answers:

Who was studying last night?

[ǰan ˈwəz]

What was John doing in his room last night?

[hi wəz ˈstədiɪŋ]

Where was John studying last night?

[hi wəz stədiɪŋ ɪn ɪz ˈrum]

When was John studying?

[hi wəz stədiɪŋ læst ˈnaɪt]

---

[1]Note to the teacher: Long English sentences may have more than one stressed word and still retain normal English rhythm. The use of the above questions and answers will help the student shift his stress automatically as the situation demands.

## PRONUNCIATION

1. Pronunciation of [m] and [n]
2. Pronunciation of [n] contrasted with [ŋ]
3. Reduced form of AS
4. Rhythm drills

### Review

a) Pronounce the following words.

|          |          |          |
|----------|----------|----------|
| [faɪ]    | [vaɪ]    | [baɪ]    |
| [fæn]    | [væn]    | [bæn]    |

b) Review the following conversations from memory.

1. Engineer A.    Are you going to visit the Ford Factory?
   Engineer B.    Yes, we're going this afternoon.
   Engineer A.    How far is it to the factory?
   Engineer B.    It's almost forty miles.

2. Student C.    Was the movie good?
   Student D.    No, it was very bad.

### 1. Pronunciation of [m] and [n]

The consonant sound [m] is a VOICED NASAL. During the pronunciation of [m] the lips are closed. The consonant [n] is a VOICED NASAL. During the pronunciation of [n] the tongue touches the tooth ridge. The stream of air comes through the nose for both of these sounds.

Notice the position of the organs of speech in the sounds [m] and [n].

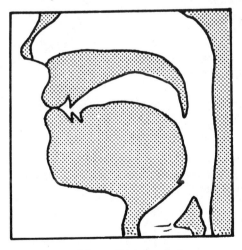

Lip position for [m]

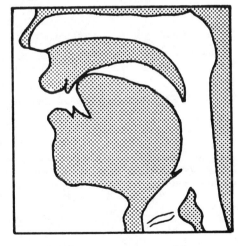

Tongue position for [n]

Pronounce the following words.

| 1 [m] | 2 [n] |
|-------|-------|
| [mæt] | [næt] |
| [mæp] | [næp] |
| [səm] | [sən] |
| [rəm] | [rən] |
| [tæm] | [tæn] |
| [ræm] | [ræn] |
| [hɛm] | [hɛn] |

Pronounce the following pair of sentences.

He wanted a cone [kon].
He wanted a comb [kom].

Pronounce the following phrases and sentences.[1]

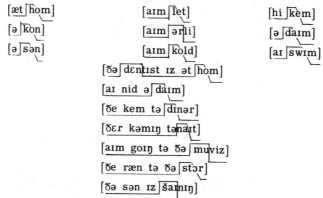

## 2. Pronunciation of [n] contrasted with [ŋ]

The sound [n] is pronounced with the tongue on the tooth ridge. The consonant [ŋ] is also a VOICED NASAL, but it is pronounced with the back of the tongue touching the velum.

Compare the following diagram with the diagram of [n] in section 1 of this lesson.

---

[1] Note to the teacher: Spanish speakers should be cautioned to close their lips completely when pronouncing [m], especially at the ends of words.

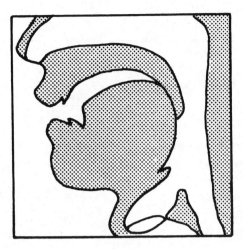

Tongue position for [ŋ]

Pronounce the following words.

|  | 1 [n] | 2 [ŋ] |
|---|---|---|
|  | [sən] | [səŋ] |
|  | [rən] | [rəŋ] |
|  | [tæn] | [tæŋ] |
|  | [ræn] | [ræŋ] |
|  | [lɔn] | [lɔŋ] |
|  | [tən] | [təŋ] |

Pronounce the following phrases and sentences.

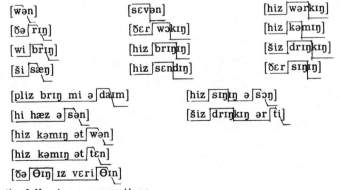

Memorize the following conversations.

Doctor A.    [du yə hæv ə ⌐mǣč⌐]

Lawyer B.    [no aɪ ⌐dont ]

Doctor A.    [ðɛrz wən an ðə⌐dɛsk pliz⌐brɪŋ⌐ ɪt tə mi]

Student F.   [hwɛr ər yə⌐gɔɪŋ]

Student G.   [aɪm goɪŋ tə⌐wɔšɪŋtən]

## 3. Reduced form of AS

Pronounce the following sentence.

[hiz əz yəŋ əz tam]                He's as young as Tom.

In normal rapid conversation the word AS [æz] is reduced to [əz]. Pronounce the following phrases and sentences with normal rapid pronunciation.

[əz⌐ɔfən əz⌐bɪl]              [əz⌐ərli əz⌐mɑri]

[əz⌐old⌐əz⌐tam]              [əz⌐sloli əz⌐gloriə]

[əz⌐fæst⌐əz⌐jɪm]              [əz⌐šɔrt⌐əz⌐jan]

[hiz əz⌐tɔl⌐əz⌐bɪl]          [ši⌐ridz⌐əz fæst əz⌐jɪm]

[hiz əz⌐larj⌐əz⌐jan]          [ðe⌐draɪv⌐əz fæst əz⌐jɪm]

[hiz əz⌐yəŋ⌐əz⌐mɛri]          [ši⌐stɑdɪz əz məč əz⌐bɪl]

[hiz əz⌐smɔl⌐əz⌐gloriə]      [wi⌐it⌐əz fæst əz ðə⌐tičər]

## 4. Rhythm drills

Pronounce the following sentences rapidly and evenly. Try to maintain an even sentence rhythm; the teacher will indicate the speed of pronunciation by tapping with his pencil.

[ðə⌐tičər gev əs ə⌐buk]

[ðə⌐mæn⌐tɔkt əbaut səm⌐kɔrsɪz]

[əlɪzəbəΘ wɛnt tə ðə⌐muviz]

[mɪsɪz⌐bartən bɔt ə nu⌐kar]

[ðə⌐student ɪz lərnɪŋ⌐ɪŋgliš]

[aɪ want səm⌐šugər ɪn maɪ⌐kɔfi]

[ši wants səm⌐bətər fər ər⌐brɛd]

[hi wants səm⌐kænɪ fər ɪz⌐sən]

[yu want səm⌐stæmps⌐fər yər⌐lɛtər]

[ðe gev əs⌐frut⌐fər ar dɪzərt]

## PRONUNCIATION

1. Pronunciation of [w]
2. Pronunciation of [g]
3. Contrast of [w] and [g]
4. Pronunciation of [y]
5. Contrast of [y] and [ʃ]
6. 2 2-4 intonation curve

Review

a) Pronounce the following words.

| [səm] | [sən] | [səŋ] |
|-------|-------|-------|
| [ræm] | [ræn] | [ræŋ] |

b) Pronounce the following sentences.

1. That thing is very thin.
2. He's coming at ten.
3. Please come in.
4. I'm going to the movies tonight.
5. She has a new comb.
6. He's singing a song.
7. When is he going?
8. He's going at seven.

c) Practice the following conversation from memory.

Doctor A.  Do you have a match?

Lawyer B.  No, I don't.

Doctor A.  There's one on the desk. Please bring it to me.

1. Pronunciation of [w]

The consonant [w] is a VOICED GLIDE[1]. At the beginning of the [w] sound the lips are rounded and the tongue is in a high back position similar to the tongue position for [u]. The lips are rapidly unrounded before the vowel which follows [w] is produced. The tongue glides smoothly into the position of the vowel which follows [w], and the voiced sound is continuous.

Notice the change in tongue and lip position during the pronunciation of [wa].

---

[1] See XI. 90

123

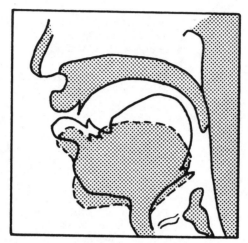

Change in tongue position for [wa]

Pronounce the following.

| | | | |
|---|---|---|---|
| [we] | [wɛr] | [want] | [wíndo] |
| [waɪf] | [wəz] | [wɛl] | [wə́ndərful] |
| [waɪd] | [wər] | [wɛnt] | [wíntər] |
| [wet] | [wərk] | [waɪnd] | [wɛ́ðər] |
| [wɔš]¹ | [wʊl] | [wɔk] | [wúmən] |
| [wɔl] | [wʊd] | [wɔrm] | [wɔr] |

[ðə ⌐wʊl ⌐ɪz ⌐wɛt]       [ðə ⌐rum ⌐hæz ə waɪd ⌐wɪndo]

[ðə ⌐wʊmən ɪz ⌐byutɪfʊl]       [ðə ⌐wɔl ɪz med əv ⌐wʊd]

[ðɪs ɪz ⌐wəndərful ⌐wɛðər]

## 2. Pronunciation of [g]

The consonant sound [g] is a VOICED STOP. During the pronunciation of [g] the back of the tongue touches the velum. Notice in the diagram that follows that the air stream is completely stopped in producing this sound.

---

¹Note to the teacher: Students must be sure to unround the lips rapidly after pronouncing [w] and before pronouncing the vowel which follows, especially before back vowels.

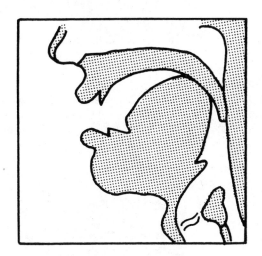

Tongue position for [g]

Pronounce the following.

| [go] | [əgέn] | [dɔg] | [šúgər] |
| [gɪv] | [bɪgín] | [lɛg] | [sɪgərét] |
| [gɛt] | [glæs] | [bɪg] | [fərgét] |

[pliz | gɪv | mi ə mægəzin]

[ðə | gərl | bɪgæn  ðə | gèm]

[ðə | gərl | hæz ə | dɔg]

[mɪsɪz | grin | wants səm | šúgər]

[aɪ ɔlwəz fərgɛt | ðə | daɪəlɔg]

[ðə | gɛst | ɪz ɪn ðə | gardən]

## 3. Contrast of [w] and [g]

When the consonant sound [w] is pronounced before a back vowel, as in WOOD, students sometimes touch the tongue to the velum. This produces a sound similar to [g] and the word resembles GOOD. Pronounce the following pairs of words. Do not touch your tongue to the velum when you pronounce [w].

| 1 [w] | 2 [g] |
|-------|-------|
| [wʊd] | [gʊd] |
| [wən] | [gən] |
| [wɔl] | [gɔl] |
| [wɔk] | [gɔk] |

Practice the following sentences.

[šiz ə wəndərful wumən]

[ðɪs wud ɪz gud]

[ðə klæs ɪz ət wən]

[wud yə gɛt mi ə sɪgərɛt]

## 4. Pronunciation of [y]

The consonant [y] is a VOICED GLIDE[1]. At the beginning of the [y] sound the tongue is in a high front position similar to the tongue position for [i]. The tongue glides smoothly into the position of the vowel sound which follows [y], and the voiced sound is continuous.

Notice the change in tongue position during the pronunciation of [ya].

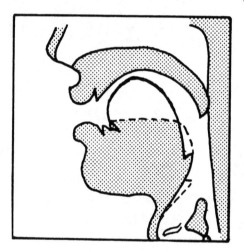

Change in tongue position for [ya]

Pronounce the following.

| | | |
|---|---|---|
| [yu] | [yɛlo] | [yéstərdi] |
| [yuz] | [yard] | [yužuəl] |
| [yɪr] | [yɛs] | [yunɪvərsɪti] |

[hi kem yɛstərdi]

[hi wɛnt tə ðə yunɪvərsɪti]

[ðə yard ɪz larǰ]

[ðə drɛs ɪz yɛlo]

---
[1]See XI. P.90

## 5. Contrast of [y] and [ǰ]

The sound [y] is pronounced without the tongue touching the tooth ridge. During the first part of the sound [ǰ] the tongue touches the tooth ridge.

Pronounce these two syllables in rapid succession.

[ya ǰa ya ǰa ya ǰa]

Pronounce the following. Be sure you do not touch the tongue to the tooth ridge when you pronounce [y].

| 1 [y] | 2 [ǰ] |
|-------|-------|
| [yu] | [ǰu] |
| [yuz] | [ǰuz] |
| [yel] | [ǰel] |
| [yɪr] | [ǰɪr] |
| [yard] | [ǰard] |
| [yɛlo] | [ǰélo] |

Practice the following conversations giving the appropriate answer.

Mr. A.  [ɪz i goɪŋ tə yel]

Mr. B.  [yɛs hiz goɪŋ tə yel]

Mr. C.  [ɪz i goɪŋ tə ǰel]

Mr. D.  [no hi ɪzənt goɪŋ tə ǰel]

Memorize the following conversation.

Dentist M.  [hwɛn dɪd yə stədi ət ðə yunɪvərsɪti]

Dentist L.  [aɪ stədɪd ðɛr læst yɪr]

Dentist M.  [du yə wənt tə go əgɛn ðɪs yɪr]

Dentist L.  [yɛs aɪ wud laɪk tu]

## 6. 2 2-4 intonation curve

Notice the intonation on the following phrases.

[ə kul de]      [ə yəŋ mæn]

In some phrases and sentences the voice frequently does not drop to pitch 3 or pitch 4 between stressed syllables, but remains on pitch 2. This is called the 2 2-4 intonation curve.

The 2 2-4 intonation is frequently heard in phrases like the following. Pronounce these phrases.

| | | | |
|---|---|---|---|
| [ə waɪd rum] | [ən old mæn] | [hi spiks ɪŋglɪš] | [ši rɛd ðə buk] |
| [ə braun kɒt] | [ə yɛlo kɒt] | [hi ridz frɛnč] | [hi sɛnt ə lɛtər] |
| [ə haɪ bɪldɪŋ] | [ə ləki bɔi] | [wi et dɪnər] | [wi sæŋ ə sɔŋ] |
| [ə larǰ klæs] | [ə brokən dɪš] | [ðe wɛnt swɪmɪŋ] | [kən yə kəm ərli] |

LESSON XVIII

PRONUNCIATION

1. Pronunciation of [l] before vowels
2. Pronunciation of [l] after vowels
3. Pronunciation of [h] and [hw]
4. Reduced forms with WILL
5. Rhythm exercises with reduced forms of HIM and HER

Review

a) Pronounce the following words.

| | | |
|---|---|---|
| wash | yes | go |
| wall | year | again |
| woman | young | garden |
| walk | yellow | dog |

b) Pronounce the following pairs of sentences

He's going to Yale.
He's going to jail.

c) Practice the following conversation from memory.

Dentist M.  When did you study at the university?
Dentist L.  I studied there last year.
Dentist M.  Would you like to go again this year?
Dentist L.  Yes, I would.

d) Pronounce the following sentences with 2 2-4 intonation as marked.

1. John is a lucky boy.

2. Can you come early?

3. We ate breakfast.

4. He's a young man.

5. It's a perfect day.

6. That's a narrow street.

7. It cost fifty cents.

8. He has brown hair.

1. Pronunciation of [l] before vowels.[1]

The consonant [l] is a VOICED LATERAL.[2] During the pronunciation of [l] before vowels, as in the word LIST, the front part of the tongue is spread out and touches the tooth ridge. The middle of the tongue is high.

Notice the position of the tongue for [l] before vowels in the diagram.

---

[1]This is sometimes called a "clear" [l] in phonetic descriptions.

[2]See XI. P. 90

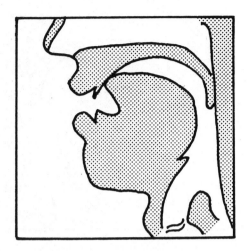

Tongue position for [l] before vowels

Pronounce the following.

| | | |
|---|---|---|
| [liv] | [laɪn] | [lɛ́sən] |
| [lɪst] | [lak] | [lɛ́tər] |
| [lɪv] | [lʊk] | [gləv] |
| [lɔŋ] | [læst] | [slo] |

[hi ʃlɛft ðə ʃhaʊs]

[aɪm ʃlʊkɪŋ fər maɪ ʃgləv]

[hiz ʃlakɪŋ ðə ʃdɔr]

[ðə ʃlæst lɛtər wəz ʃlɔŋ]

[ðə ʃlaɪn ɪz vɛri ʃlɔŋ]

2. Pronunciation of [l] after vowels[1]

During the pronunciation of [l] after vowels, as in CALL, the tip of the tongue touches the tooth ridge. The middle of the tongue is low.

Notice the position of the tongue for [l] after vowels in the diagram.

---

[1] This is sometimes called a "dark" [l] in phonetic descriptions.

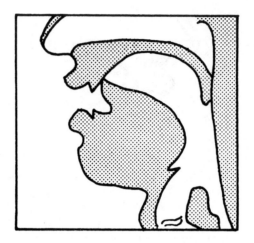

Tongue position for [l] after vowels

Pronounce the following. Make a slow transition between the vowel and the [l] and keep the middle of the tongue low.[1]

| | | |
|---|---|---|
| [il] | [pil] | [pul] |
| [el] | [pel] | [pol] |
| [æl] | [pæl] | [kol] |
| [ɔl] | [pɔl] | [hɔl] |
| [ɪl] | [dəl] | [mɪlk] |
| [ɛl] | [dal] | [hɛlp] |
| [fɪl] | [ful] | [fɛlt] |
| [fɛl] | [sɛl] | [šɛlf] |

| | |
|---|---|
| an early fall | all of the meal |
| a cold hall | all of the wool |
| a tall child | all of the bill |
| a pale child | all of the milk |
| a small pill | all of the wall |

[hi fɪlz ˺kòld]            [ðə čaɪld ɪz vɛri ˺tɔ̀l]

[šiz ɪn ðə ˺hɔ̀l]          [ðə mɪlk ɪz vɛri ˺kòld]

[ðə mɪlk ɪz ˺gùd]

---

[1] For a fuller description of this technique applied to Spanish-speakers and others who use a "clear" [l] after vowels, see article by Betty J. Wallace, LANGUAGE LEARNING, Volume I, Number 2, pp. 24-25.

Memorize the following conversations

Doctor.       [mɪstər ⌐wɪlsən ɪz ⌐ɪl   wɪl yə ⌐hɛlp⌐ ɪm]

Student.      [yɛs aɪ ⌐wɪl]

Professor S.  [haʊ dʊ yə ⌐fil]

Professor T.  [aɪ fil ⌐faɪn]

Lawyer B.     [haʊ dʊ yə ⌐fil]

Lawyer C.     [aɪ dont ⌐fil⌐ vɛri wɛl]

## 3. Pronunciation of [h] and [hw]

The consonant [h] is a GLIDE.[1] It is produced by aspiration before a vowel. During the pronunciation of [h] the tongue and lips are in the position for the pronunciation of the vowel which follows [h]. For example, for [hu] the tongue is in a high back position and the lips are rounded; for [hi] the tongue is in a high front position and the lips are unrounded. The sound [h] is voiceless; voicing is added in order to pronounce the vowel which follows [h].[2]

Pronounce the following.

| | | | |
|---|---|---|---|
| [hat] | [hɔt] | [hə́ŋgri] | [hǽpən] |
| [het] | [hæt] | [hə́zbənd] | [hɛ́lθi] |
| [hit] | [hɪt] | [hǽnsəm] | [hɛ́dek] |

[hiz ɪn ðə ⌐hɔl]

[hiz ɪn ðə ⌐haʊs]

[hər həzbənd ɪz ⌐hɪr]

[ðɛr ⌐həŋgri]

[ðɛr ⌐hɛlθi]

In the sound [hw] the tongue and lips are in the position for [w]. In rapid pronunciation when a word begins with the sound [hw] the aspiration is often omitted, especially when the word is not stressed.[3]

Pronounce the following.

| | |
|---|---|
| [hwɔt] | [hwətɛ́vər] |
| [hwɛn] | [hwɛrɛ́vər] |
| [hwɛr] | [hwɛnɛ́vər] |
| [hwaɪ] | [hwaɪl] |

---

[1] See XI.P.90

[2] Many Spanish-speakers pronounce [h] with a strong fricative sound at the velum as in Spanish JARRO. There should not be such strong friction in the English [h] sound.

[3] Note to the teacher. Many English speakers make no distinction between [w] and [hw].

[hwətɛvər i︤ hæz]                          [wətɛvər i︤ hæz]

[hwaɪl iz ︤ hɪr]                              [waɪl iz ︤ hɪr]

[hwən dɪd i︤ kəm]                          [wɛn dɪd i︤ kəm]

[hwɛr dɪd i︤ go]                            [wɛr dɪd i︤ go]

[hwət dɪd i︤ hæv]                          [wət dɪd i︤ hæv]

Memorize the following conversation.

John.    [hwɛr ɪz ər︤ həzbənd]

James.   [hiz ɪn ðə︤ haʊs]

## 4. Reduced forms with will

Pronounce the following pair of sentences.

[wi wɪl go︤ letər]                          [wɪl go︤ letər]

[wi wɪl bi︤ let]                             [wɪl bi︤ let]

In normal rapid pronunciation the word WILL is combined with other words to produce the following reduced forms.

| you will | [yul] |
| they will | [ðel] |
| she will | [šil] |
| he will | [hil] |
| I will | [aɪl] |
| it will | [ítəl] |
| we will | [wil] |
| John will | [ǰánəl] |
| Mary will | [mɛ́riəl] |

Pronounce the following sentences using the reduced forms of WILL.

[yul go︤ letər]                             [ðel bi ðɛr︤ letər]

[ðel go︤ letər]                             [wil bi ðɛr︤ letər]

[šil go︤ letər]                             [yul bi ðɛr︤ letɛr]

[hil go︤ letər]                             [mɛriəl əɪ bi ðɛr︤ letər]

[ǰanəl go︤ letər]                           [aɪl bi ðɛr︤ letər]

## 5. Rhythm exercises with reduced forms of him and her

The teacher will ask the questions in the following exercise. Give the answers with normal rapid pronunciation using the reduced forms of HIM and HER [ɪm] and [ər].

[dɪd yə mit mɪstər︤ smɪθ]                   [yɛs aɪ mɛt ɪm︤ yɛstərdi]

[dɪd yə mit mɪs︤ ændərsən]                  [yɛs aɪ mɛt ər︤ yɛstərdi]

[dɪd yə mit ⌐mɛ˩ri]

[dɪd yə mit ⌐ra˩bərt]

[dɪd yə mit ⌐ǰan]

[dɪd yə mit ə˩lɪzəbɛɵ]

[dɪd yə mit ⌐ǰan]

[dɪd yə mit ə˩lɪzəbɛɵ]

[dɪd yə mit ⌐ra˩bərt]

[dɪd yə mit ⌐mɛ˩ri]

[dɪd yə mit mɪstər ⌐smɪɵ]

[dɪd yə mit ⌐ǰemz]

[ȳɛs aɪ mɛt ər ⌐yɛs˩tərdi]

[ȳɛs aɪ mɛt ɪm ⌐yɛs˩tərdi]

[ȳɛs aɪ mɛt ɪm ⌐yɛs˩tərdi]

[ȳɛs aɪ mɛt ər ⌐yɛs˩tərdi]

[n̄o aɪ dɪdnt ⌐mit˩ ɪm]

[n̄o aɪ dɪdnt ⌐mit˩ ər]

[n̄o aɪ dɪdnt ⌐mit˩ ɪm]

[n̄o aɪ dɪdnt ⌐mit˩ ər]

[n̄o aɪ dɪdnt ⌐mit˩ ɪm]

[n̄o aɪ dɪdnt ⌐mit˩ ɪm]

## PRONUNCIATION

1. Pronunciation of [p], [t], and [k]
2. Syllabic consonants [n] and [l]
3. Rhythm drills with DIDN'T, COULDN'T, SHOULDN'T, WOULDN'T
4. Reduced forms of HAVE TO, HAS TO, USED TO
5. Rhythm drills

Review

a) Pronounce the following words.

| | | | |
|---|---|---|---|
| leave | slow | pale | milk |
| last | glove | child | help |
| long | lesson | hall | felt |
| line | letter | wool | cold |

b) Practice the following conversations from memory.

Professor S. How do you feel?
Professor T. I feel fine.

John. Where is her husband?
James. He's in the house.

c) Pronounce the following sentences using the reduced forms of WILL, and HIM and HER.

1. He'll talk to you tomorrow.
2. They'll go to Detroit next week.
3. I gave her the book yesterday.
4. They told him about the movie.
5. I didn't ask her.

1. Pronunciation of [p], [t], and [k]

The sounds [p], [t], and [k] are VOICELESS STOPS. During the pronunciation of [p] the lips are together. During the pronunciation of [t] the front of the tongue touches the tooth ridge. During the pronunciation of [k] the middle of the tongue touches the velum.

Notice the position of the lips and tongue for the pronunciation of [p], [t] and [k] in the diagrams below.

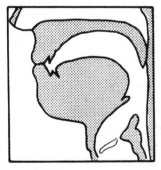 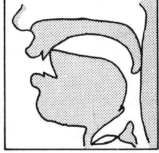 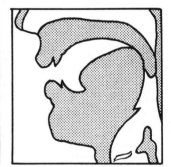

Lip position for [p]        Tongue position for [t]        Tongue position for [k]

134

When the consonants [p], [t] and [k] are at the beginning of stressed syllables, they are pronounced with slight aspiration; that is, there is a small [h] sound between the consonant and vowel which follows it.[1]

Pronounce the following words with aspiration after [p], [t] and [k].

| [paɪ] | [tébəl] | [kar] |
|---|---|---|
| [pɛn] | [tǽksi] | [kǽndi] |
| [pɛr] | [test] | [kold] |
| [paʊnd] | [tɔk] | [kɔfi] |
| [paɪp] | [tɛl] | [kəm] |
| [pípəl] | [tost] | [kæš] |

When the consonants [p], [t] and [k] occur at the end of a syllable or in unstressed position they are pronounced with no aspiration. Pronounce the following words. Do not aspirate [p], [t] and [k] when they occur at the end of a syllable or in unstressed position. (As in the second column.)

[p]

| [pípəl] | [slip] |
|---|---|
| [paʊnd] | [hop] |
| [əpríšiet] | [kæmpəs] |
| [əpártmənt] | [haspɪtəl] |
| [ɛkspɛ́ns] | [kip] |

[t]

| [tébəl] | [hit] |
|---|---|
| [ətɛ́nd] | [sɪt] |
| [tost] | [raɪt] |
| [ətrǽkšən] | [kəstəm] |
| [test] | [daktər] |

[k]

| [kar] | [lek] |
|---|---|
| [kəm] | [smok] |
| [kæš] | [pakɪt] |
| [ɪnkrís] | [pɪknɪk] |
| [bɪkə́m] | [nɪkəl] |

Pronounce the following sentences.

[ðə ⌐tost ɪz ⌐hat]

[ðə ⌐pípəl wər əslíp]

[hi hæz ə ⌐paɪp ɪn ɪz ⌐pakɪt]

[ðə ⌐kæmpəs wəz ⌐kul]

[ðə kɔfi wəz ⌐kold]

---

[1]Note to the teacher: Spanish-speakers can sometimes be made aware of the difference between Spanish and English [p] by pronouncing in contrast PIPA in Spanish and [paɪp] in English with a lighted match held before the mouth.

[pliz|tɛl|mi ðə|faɪm]

[ðə|pɪkɲɪk wəz|ɪntrɪstɪŋ]

[hi nɪdɪd ən əpartmənt]

Memorize the following conversations.

|  |  |
|---|---|
| Clerk. | [du yə want⌐kɔfi ər⌐ti] |
| Student. | [aɪ want⌐ti|pliz] |
| Clerk. | [du yə want⌐šugər ɪn yər ti (kɔfi)] |
| | |
| Engineer A. | [du yə hæv ə⌐pɛnsəl] |
| Engineer B. | [yɛs ɪts ɪn ðə⌐pakɪt əv maɪ⌐kot] |
| | |
| Lawyer L. | [du yə hæv ə⌐kar] |
| Lawyer L. | [yɛs aɪ hæv ə⌐kædɪlæk] |
| Lawyer L. | [ðæts ə vɛri ɛkspɛnsɪv kar] |
| Lawyer M. | [yɛs bət ɪts vɛri|kəmftəbəl] |

## 2. Syllabic Consonants [n] and [l]

Some consonants, especially the continuants, are often syllabic; that is, the consonant itself is the center of a syllable, or it is an entire syllable in itself; the vowel which precedes it is omitted entirely. The instructor will pronounce the two following columns of words. Observe the vowel in the second syllable of each word in column A; observe the omission of the vowel in the second syllable of the same word in Column B.

| A. | B. |
|---|---|
| [lítəl] | [lítl] |
| [tótəl] | [tótl] |
| [pə́rsən] | [pə́rsn] |
| [studənt] | [stúdnt] |

Observe that the vowel which is omitted is [ə]. In this text the vowel which is pronounced in words with syllabic consonants has been included in the phonetic representation of words.

Two of the consonants most frequently pronounced as syllabic consonants are [l] and [n] in unstressed syllables.

Pronounce the following two columns of words. Observe the omission of the vowel in each word in the second column. Pronounce the consonant that remains as a syllabic consonant.

[l]

| | |
|---|---|
| [lɪtəl] | [lɪtl] |
| [batəl] | [bátl] |
| [pɛnsəl] | [pɛ́nsl] |
| [ɛksələnt] | [ɛkslənt] |
| [haspɪtəl] | [háspɪtl] |

[n]

| | |
|---|---|
| [gárdən] | [gárdn] |
| [lɛ́sən] | [lɛ́sn] |
| [wílsən] | [wílsn] |
| [sə́rtənli] | [sə́rtnlɪ] |
| [ɪmpɔ́rtənt] | [ɪmpɔ́rtnt] |

Observe also that the word AND is frequently reduced to a syllabic [n].

| | |
|---|---|
| [brɛd ənd bətər] | [brɛd n bətər] |
| [bɔɪz ənd gərlz] | [bɔɪz n gərlz] |
| [hi sɪŋz ənd dænsɪz] | [hɪ sɪŋz n dænsɪz] |
| [ðɪs ənd ðæt] | [ðɪs n ðæt] |
| [mɪstər bartən ən ǰan] | [mɪstər bartən n ǰan] |

The reduced forms DIDN'T, COULDN'T, WOULDN'T, SHOULDN'T, ISN'T, WASN'T are often pronounced with syllabic [n]. Pronounce the following sentences.[1]

| | |
|---|---|
| [hi dɪdnt go] | [hi wudnt go] |
| [ši kudnt go] | [ðe šudnt go] |
| [hi ɪznt ə student] | [ši ɪznt ə tičər] |
| [ši wəznt ə student] | [hi wəznt ə tičər] |

Practice the following sentences. Use the syllabic consonant [l] or [n] whenever possible.

1. The speech was excellent.
2. The book is important.
3. The students are coming tomorrow.
4. She has a beautiful garden.
5. They didn't want the books.
6. The boys and girls are here.
7. It's in the middle of the lesson.
8. We had bread and butter for supper.

Memorize the following conversations.

Teacher: [ɪz ðə lɛsən ɪmpɔrtənt]

Student: [yɛs ɪt sərtənli ɪz]

Teacher: [hwɛr ɪz mɪstər wɪlsən]

Student: [hiz æbsənt təde]

3. Rhythm drills with DIDN'T, COULDN'T, SHOULDN'T, WOULDN'T

---

[1]The symbol [ə] has been omitted here for purposes of drill.

Pronounce the following sentences with smooth sentence rhythm. Use the syllabic [n] in the words DIDN'T, COULDN'T, SHOULDN'T, WOULDN'T.

[hi dɪdnt ˈlɪsən tə mi]                [ðe dɪdnt ˈrid ɪt]

[hi šudnt lɪsən tə mi]                [ðe šudnt rid ɪt]

[hi kudnt lɪsən tə mi]               [ðe kudnt rid ɪt]

[hi wudnt lɪsən tə mi]               [ðe wudnt rid ɪt]

[hi dɪdnt fərgɛt ɪt]                  [hi dɪdnt ˈluk ət ər]

[hi šudnt fərgɛt ɪt]                  [hi šudnt luk ət ər]

[hi kudnt fərgɛt ɪt]                 [hi kudnt luk ət ər]

[hi wudnt fərgɛt ɪt]                [hi wudnt luk ət ər]

4. <u>Reduced forms of HAVE TO, HAS TO, USED TO.</u>

Pronounce the following.

[aɪ hæf tə stədi]            I have to study.

[aɪ hæf tə it]               I have to eat.

[hi hæs tə wərk]           He has to work.

[hi hæs tə rid]             He has to read.

[aɪ yus tə stədi]           I used to study.

[hi yus tə rid]            He used to read.

Notice the difference between the reduced form and the full form of the following expressions.

|  | Full Form | Reduced Form |
|---|---|---|
| have to | [hæv tu] | [hæftə] |
| has to | [hæz tu] | [hæstə] |
| used to | [yuz tu] | [yustə] |

Pronounce the following with normal rapid pronunciation.

[hi hæs tə go tə ðɪ ɔfɪs]

[hi yus tə go tə ðə kansərts]

[wi hæf tə spik ɪŋgliš]

[ðe yus tə wərk ɪn ðə laɪbrɛri]

[wi yus tə smok]

[ši hæs tə kəm ərli]

[aɪ hæf tə go tə klæs]

[ðe hæf tə it lənč nau]

[du yə hæf tə ⌐go⌐ nau]

[wi yus tə drɪŋk ⌐kɔfi]

## 5. Rhythm drills

Read the following series of sentences with smooth sentence rhythm. The teacher will indicate the speed of pronunciation by tapping with a pencil. Pronounce the sentences so that the interval between the stresses does not change.

a)  [yu kən ⌐faɪnd⌐ ɪt]

   [yu kən ⌐faɪnd⌐ ɪt ɪn ðɪ ɛnsaɪkləpidɪə]

   [yu kən ⌐faɪnd⌐ ɪt ɪn ðə larʃ ɛnsaɪkləpidɪə]

   [yu kən ⌐faɪnd⌐ ɪt ɪn ðə larʃ ɛnsaɪkləpidɪə ɪn ðə ⌐laɪbrɛri]

b)  [aɪm goɪŋ tə⌐stədi]

   [aɪm goɪŋ tə⌐stədi ɪn maɪ ⌐rum]

   [aɪm goɪŋ tə⌐stədi ɪn maɪ ⌐rum⌐ wɪð ə⌐frɛnd]

   [aɪm goɪŋ tə⌐stədi ɪn maɪ ⌐rum⌐ wɪð ə⌐frɛnd⌐ ðæt yə⌐no]

c)  [aɪ kudnt ⌐go]

   [aɪ kudnt ⌐go tə ðə⌐stɔr]

   [aɪ kudnt ⌐go tə ðə⌐stɔr baɪ ⌐kar]

   [aɪ kudnt ⌐go tə ðə⌐stɔr baɪ ⌐kar yɛstərde]

d)  [hi yus tə it⌐hæmbərgərz]

   [hi yus tə it⌐hæmbərgərz æt ə⌐drəg⌐stɔr]

   [hi yus tə it⌐hæmbərgərz æt ə⌐drəg⌐stɔr wɪð ə⌐studnt]

   [hi yus tə it⌐hæmbərgərz æt ə⌐drəg⌐stɔr wɪð ə⌐studnt frəm yur⌐klæs]

e)  [dəz i hæf tə⌐wərk]

   [dəz i hæf tə⌐wərk ɪn ðə⌐gardn]

   [dəz i hæf tə⌐wərk ɪn ðə⌐gardn wɪð ɪz⌐faðər]

   [dəz i hæf tə⌐wərk ɪn ðə⌐gardn wɪð ɪz⌐faðər ðɪz æftərnun]

## LESSON XX

### PRONUNCIATION

1. Review of vowels
2. Review of consonants
3. Stress and intonation
4. Practice on forms of the verbs
5. Practice on CAN, CAN'T, and DIDN'T
6. Practice on IT'S and THERE'S

1. Review of vowels

a) Pronounce the vowel sounds from the chart below.

| | | | | |
|---|---|---|---|---|
| 1. | [i] | | [u] | 8. |
| 2. | [ɪ] | | [ʊ] | 9. |
| 3. | [e] | (6) | [o] | 10. |
| 4. | [ɛ] | [ə] | | |
| 5. | [æ] | (7) [a] | [ɔ] | 11. |

b) Identify the vowel sound of the following words by number from the vowel chart.

| do | sit | is | put | say | take | speak |
|---|---|---|---|---|---|---|
| come | get | sell | know | teach | leave | make |
| meet | cost | go | think | eat | see | bring |

c) Give the past form of the words in section (b) and identify the vowel sound.

d) Pronounce the following sentences.

1. He sleeps late.
2. The examination is easy.
3. He lives in the city.
4. The man is in class.
5. The class begins at eight o'clock.
6. He has a lot of money.
7. He bought a small boat.
8. The food is usually good.
9. Robert is a rapid reader.
10. He's hungry.

2. Review of consonants

Pronounce the following sentences.

1. He's playing volley ball.
2. Miss Smith is asleep.
3. Ships are boats.
4. Sheep are animals.
5. Potato chips are good to eat.
6. Jeeps are automobiles.
7. Blue jeans are cheap.
8. He's in room eleven at the Rackham Building.
9. The sun usually shines.

140

10. He's as young as John.
11. What time is it? It's ten minutes to two.
12. How do you feel? I feel fine, thank you.
13. This lesson is very important.
14. He lives at 179 Main Street.
15. He likes to smoke.

## 3. Stress and intonation

a) Pronounce the following sentences emphasizing the words which the teacher tells you. Use 2-3 2-4 intonation

1. The man is going to the movies.
2. They went to a concert in the evening.
3. We often attend the lectures in the auditorium.
4. The professor can answer the question.
5. She smiles at the students in the class.

b) Practice the following conversation with the intonation as marked.

John:   Would you like to go to the movies?

Robert: Yes, I would.

John:   Good, let's go.

## 4. Practice on forms of the verbs

a) Pronounce the following sentence.

I WALK and she WALKS too.

Substitute the following words or phrases for WALK in the above sentence.

| | | |
|---|---|---|
| run | laugh at him | wash the dishes |
| smile | point at him | read English |
| study | talk to him | speak English |
| understand | listen to him | watch the baby |

b) Pronounce the following sentence.

He said, "WALK," and I WALKED.

Substitute the words and phrases from section (a) in this sentence.

## 5. Practice on CAN, CAN'T, and DIDN'T

a) Pronounce the following with smooth sentence rhythm.

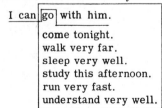

I can go with him.
come tonight.
walk very far.
sleep very well.
study this afternoon.
run very fast.
understand very well.

b) Substitute the phrase from section (a) in the following sentences.

I can't _____ .

I didn't _____ .

## 6. Practice on IT'S and THERE'S

Pronounce the following sentences with normal rapid pronunciation. Be sure you use the reduced forms IT'S and THERE'S.

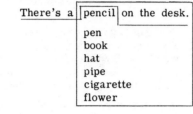

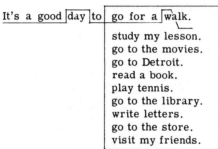

## LESSON XXI

### PRONUNCIATION

1. Phonetic syllabication
2. Marking pauses for rhythm and intonation
3. Review of [i] and [ɪ]

## 1. Phonetic syllabication[1]

Pronounce the following phrases.

| | | |
|---|---|---|
| did it | drive it | cause it |
| like it | catch it | close it |
| make it | expect it | open it |
| stop it | discuss it | move it |
| keep it | change it | contain it |

Notice how each phrase is pronounced as one unit. The final consonant of the first word tends to become the initial consonant of the second word when the second word begins with a vowel. This is called phonetic syllabication.

| | | |
|---|---|---|
| [dɪd ɪt] | becomes | [dɪ - dɪt] |
| [laɪk ɪt] | becomes | [laɪ - kɪt] |

Pronounce the following phrases.

| | | |
|---|---|---|
| closed it | helped it | brushed it |
| caused it | stopped it | cashed it |
| opened it | discussed it | liked it |
| moved it | left it | ordered it |
| changed it | kept it | watched it |

Notice how each phrase is pronounced as one unit. The final consonant of the first word tends to become the initial consonant of the second word when the second word begins with a vowel. This simplifies many of the complex combinations of consonants which occur in English.

| | | |
|---|---|---|
| [klozd ɪt] | becomes | [kloz - dɪt] |
| [kɔzd ɪt] | becomes | [kɔz - dɪt] |

Practice the following phrases. Pronounce each phrase as a unit, but put the final consonants of the first word of the phrase at the beginning of the next word, if that word begins with a vowel sound.

For example: [staps æt hom] becomes [stap - sæt hom]

| | | |
|---|---|---|
| stops at home | smiles at her | girls in here |
| left at home | laughs at her | students in here |
| lived at home | looks at her | dentists in here |
| helps at home | points at her | doctors in here |

Pronounce the following sentences using phonetic syllabication wherever possible.

---

[1] This term is taken from T. Navarro Tomas and Aurelio M. Espinosa, A PRIMER OF SPANISH PRONUNCIATION, Benjamin H. Sanborn and Company, New York, 1926, p. 7 ff.

   1. John was tired of reading.
   2. They changed all of the questions.
   3. The parts of the country I like best are in the West.
   4. He always turns on the radio.
   5. He learned all of the words.
   6. The teachers worked all day.
   7. All of the dentists are in their offices.
   8. They arranged our program.
   9. She washed all of the dishes.
   10. They stopped at the hotel.

Memorize the following conversations. Notice the phonetic syllabication.

   Student A.    [hwɛn‖mɛri fərst əraɪvd‖hɪr ši dɪdənt‖laɪk‖ðɪs‖sɪti]

   Student B.    [dəz ši laɪ-kɪt naʊ]

   Student A.    [yɛs ši čenǰ-dər‖maɪnd]

Pronounce the following sentences using phonetic syllabication wherever possible.

                        It's a --------
                        [ɪt-sa -------]

It's a new book.                      It's an easy examination.
It's a good answer.                   It's a good typewriter.
It's an interesting question.         It's an intelligent answer.
It's a beautiful day.                 It's a large box.

                        There's a ----
                        [ðɛr-zə -----]

There's a book on the table.          There's a doctor in my class.
There's a pencil in the drawer.       There's a boat on the river.
There's a dollar in my purse.         There's a Colombian in the course.
There's a suit in the closet.         There's a teacher in the room.

                        That's a -----
                        [ðæt-sa -----]

That's a man in my English class.     That's a little boy in the car.
That's a new book on the table.       That's an interesting story.
That's a piece of chalk.              That's an exciting mystery.
That's a picture of my mother.        That's a difficult question.
That's a new automobile.              That's a new coat.

## 2. Marking pauses for rhythm and intonation

The purpose of this exercise is to practice dividing sentences into groups. Pause after each word that you emphasize. Use 2-3 2-4 intonation.

a) Mark pauses with a bar [/] in the following sentences. There should be 3 groups of words in each sentence.

Example: The man/ is going/ to the movies./

   1. John is coming to Ann Arbor.
   2. The boy is going to study at the university.
   3. The students like to go to concerts.

4. The professor can answer the questions.
5. Many doctors are studying at the university.
6. The lawyers read many books in the library.
7. The doctors are young and enthusiastic.
8. They attend the lectures in the auditorium.
9. The students receive many letters in the morning.
10. The teacher smiled at the students in class.

b) Notice the difference in the following sentences.

The man/ is going/ to the movies./

The man/ is going to the movies./

Pronounce the sentences in section (a) with only 2 groups of words by omitting one pause as in the example above.

3. Review of [i] and [ɪ]

Pronounce the following. Make a clear distinction between [i] and [ɪ].

|          |          |
|----------|----------|
| [pɪn]    | [wik]    |
| [kin]    | [dɪd]    |
| [sil]    | [sim]    |
| [pɪl]    | [dɪd]    |

[hiz ˈitɪŋ]

[hiz ˈslipɪŋ]

[hiz ˈridɪŋ]

[hiz ˈslɪpɪŋ]

Memorize the following conversation.

Doctor A.    [ɪz i ˈslipɪŋ]
Doctor B.    [no hiz itɪŋ ˈdɪnər]

## LESSON XXII

### PRONUNCIATION

1. Consonant clusters with [r] after vowels
2. Consonant clusters with [r] before vowels
3. Intonation exercise. "The Purple Cow"
4. Exercise in marking pauses

Review

a) Pronounce the following sentences. Use phonetic syllabication when the words are underlined.

1. I stopped him.
2. She asked her a question.
3. There's a new book on the table.
4. The doctors are early.
5. She arranged our program.

b) Practice the following conversation from memory.

Student A. When Mary first arrived here, she didn't like this city.
Student B. Does she like it now?
Student A. Yes. She changed her mind.

c) Practice the following conversation from memory. Which words contain the sound [i]? Which words contain the sound [ɪ]?

Doctor A. Is he sleeping?
Doctor B. No. He's eating dinner.

1. Consonant clusters with [r] after vowels

It is important to remember that the [r] sound is pronounced without contact or vibration against the top of the mouth. Pronounce the following sounds. Concentrate on the correct pronunciation of [r].

| | | | | | |
|---|---|---|---|---|---|
| [ərz] | [ɔrz] | [ɪrz] | [ɔrd] | [ard] | [ərd] |
| [ərv] | [ərb] | [ɔrt] | [ərt] | [ərn] | |
| [ərnz] | [ərts] | [ərks] | [ərbz] | [arts] | |

a) Pronounce the simple form and the plural of the following words.

Example:  [wərd]  [wərdz]

| | | |
|---|---|---|
| [stɔr] | [dínər] | [yard] |
| [yɪr] | [fáðər] | [stǽndərd] |
| [kar] | [wíntər] | [kard] |
| [dɔr] | [sə́mər] | [wərd] |

b) Pronounce the simple form and third person singular of the following words.

Example:  [wɛr]  [wɛrz]

| | | |
|---|---|---|
| [hɪr] | [sərv] | [lərn] |
| [ɔ́rdər] | [kərv] | [ərn] |
| [hwíspər] | [rɪzə́rv] | [rɪtə́rn] |
| [kə́vər] | | [kənsə́rn] |
| | | [tərn] |

146

c) Pronounce the simple form and the past form of the following words.

Example:  [ɔrdər]  [ɔrdərd]

| | | |
|---|---|---|
| [ɔfər] | [ædmaɪr] | [rɪtərn] |
| [ænsər] | [rɪkwaɪr] | [lərn] |
| [ɔrdər] | [prɪpɛr] | [kənsə́rn] |
| [inkwáɪr] | [prɪfər] | [tərn] |

d) Pronounce the following words.

| | | |
|---|---|---|
| [hərt] | [part] | [hərts] |
| [kwɔrt] | [vərb] | [parts] |
| [kánsərt] | [wərk] | [vərbz] |

Practice the following sentences.

[ðe prɪfərd ðə wɛðər ɪn ðə səmər]

[wi ərnd ə lat əv məni]

[ðɛr wər mɛni karz an ðə strit]

[ðə stɔrz ar an men strit]

[hi hwɪspərd ðɪ ænsər]

Practice the difference between the following sentences.[1]

The teachers work in the morning.
The teacher works in the morning.

Memorize the following conversation.

Dentist C.  [hæv yu ɔrdərd ar dɪnər]

Dentist D.  [yɛs ənd aɪ ɔlso ɔrdərd dɪzərt]

## 2. Consonant clusters with [r] before vowels

Practice the following combinations with [r] before vowels. Be sure not to touch the tip of the tongue to the top of your mouth. Round the lips for the [r] before pronouncing consonants preceding [r], except [p] and [b].

| | | | | | | |
|---|---|---|---|---|---|---|
| [prə][2] | [trə] | [krə] | [brə] | [grə] | [strə] | [sprə] |
| [pr] | | | [tr] | | | [kr] |
| [praɪs] | | | [tre] | | | [krim] |
| [prógræm] | | | [traɪ] | | | [kraɪm] |
| [prɛ́zɪdənt] | | | [tri] | | | |
| [prɪfə́r] | | | [truθ] | | | [ɪnkrís] |

---

[1]Note to the teacher: For an explanation of the use of this exercise see the introduction to this volume.

[2]If necessary pronounce this first with an extra vowel between the two consonants: [pərə], [tərə], etc.

[prábləm]                    [tru]                    [dəskraɪb]
[prǽktɪs]                                             [prɪskraɪb]
[príti]                      [kəntrol]                [dɪskrípšən]
[prəvaɪd]                    [ɔ́rkɛstrə]
                             [əléktrɪk]
[témprəčər]                  [ətrǽktɪv]
[ɪmprúv]                     [ɪntrədəkšən]
[ɛkspréšən]

         [br]                        [dr]                        [gr]

[brɛd]                       [drɪŋk]                  [grup]
[brɪŋ]                       [drəg stɔr]              [gred]
[brek]                       [drɛs]                   [grin]
[brəš]                       [draɪv]                  [gro]
[briδ]                       [drəgɪst]
                                                      [prəgrɛ́s]

         [spr]                       [str]

[sprɪŋ]                      [strit]
[sprɔl]                      [strɪkt]
[spre]                       [stret]

Memorize the following conversations.

Student L.    [ar yə ̂ həŋgri]

Student M.    [yɛs aɪ ̂ æm]

Student L.    [lɛts gɛt səm aɪs ̂ krim]

Engineer A.   [ɪts dɪ̂fɪkəlt tə ɪmpruv ar prənənsiéšən]

Engineer B.   [yɛ̄s wi ̂ nid ə lat əv ̂ prǽktɪs]

John.         [huz yər ̂ frɛnd šiz vɛri ətrǽktɪv]

Jim.          [hər nem ɪz ̂ frǽnsɪs aɪ mɛt ər æt δə ̂ prógræm]

## 3. Intonation exercise

The instructor will read the following poem. Read it rapidly and smoothly as marked. Emphasize only the words marked. Memorize the poem.

### The Purple Cow

#### Gelett Burgess

I never ̂ saw ̂ a purple ̂ cow,

I never ̂ hope ̂ to ̂ see ̂ one;

But I can ̂ tell ̂ you ̂ anyhow,

I'd rather ̂ see ̂ than ̂ be ̂ one.

## 4. Exercise in marking pauses

Mark the following paragraph for acceptable rhythm as the first sentence is marked. Read the paragraph after you mark it.

There was a picnic/ at a farm/ in the country yesterday./ All of the students were invited to the picnic. They drove to Dr. Peter's farm, which is several miles from the city. The part of the farm the students enjoyed most was the lake. The lake was about a mile long and a half mile wide. The students swam in the lake and ate dinner beside the lake. They returned home about eight o'clock in the evening, and they all slept well that night.

## LESSON XXIII

## PRONUNCIATION

1. Consonant clusters with [m]
2. Consonant clusters with [n]
3. Consonant clusters with [ŋ]
4. Exercise in marking pauses
5. Practice on the reduced forms of
   COULD HAVE, SHOULD HAVE,
   MIGHT HAVE, WOULD HAVE.

## Review

a) Practice the difference between the following sentences.

The doctor<u>s</u> <u>learn</u> the new vocabulary.
The doct<u>or</u> <u>learns</u> the new vocabulary.

b) Practice the following conversations from memory.

Dentist C. Have you ordered dinner?
Dentist D. Yes, and I also ordered dessert.

John.   Who's your friend? She's very attractive.
Jim.    Her name is Frances. I met her at the program.

c) Practice the following poem with suitable intonation.

I never saw a purple cow,
I never hope to see one;
But I can tell you, anyhow,
I'd rather see than be one.

## 1. Consonant clusters with [m]

In the pronunciation of [m] the lips are completely closed. Pronounce the following words.

| 1 | 2 | 3 |
|---|---|---|
| [taɪ] | [taɪm] | [taɪmz] |
| [ar] | [arm] | [armz] |
| [ru] | [rum] | [rumz] |
| [fɔr] | [fɔrm] | [fɔrmz] |
| [ne] | [nem] | [nemz] |
| [wɔr] | [wɔrm] | [wɔrmz] |

Pronounce the following syllables. Be sure your lips are completely closed when pronouncing [m].

[amz]   [emd]   [aɪmz]   [əmz]   [ɪmz]   [ɔrmd]

Pronounce the following words.

| | | |
|---|---|---|
| [daɪmz] | [rumd] | [sə́mtaɪmz] |
| [kəmz] | [farmd] | [níknemz] |
| [swɪmz] | [fɔrmd] | [prógræmz] |
| [simz] | [nemd] | [prábləmz] |
| [nemz] | [simd] | [bɛ́drumz] |

150

Practice the following sentences.

[ðə| prǿgræmz ar ɪmpɔ́rtənt]

[ðə| lɛ́sən ɪz səmtaɪmz| dɪ́fɪkəlt]

[ðɛr| kə́stəmz ar| dɪ́frənt]

[ðə| rumz| ar vɛri| lárǰ]

Practice the difference between the following pairs of sentences.[1]

1.  [ðə| nemz| sim| dɪ́fɪkəlt]

    [ðə| nem| simz| dɪ́fɪkəlt]

2.  [ðə| rumz| sim| byútɪful]

    [ðə| rum| simz| byútɪful]

## 2. Consonant clusters with [n]

The sound [n] is pronounced with the tongue against the tooth ridge. Pronounce the following words.

| 1 | 2 | 3 |
|---|---|---|
| [si] | [sin] | [sinz] |
| [faɪ] | [faɪn] | [faɪnz] |
| [le] | [len] | [lenz] |
| [lo] | [lon] | [lonz] |
| [lɔ] | [lɔn] | [lɔnz] |

Practice the following syllables. Be sure your tongue is touching the tooth ridge when you pronounce [n].

[ənz]    [ənd]    [aɪnz]    [aɪnd]    [ɪnz]    [ond]

[ənts]   [ænts]   [aunts]   [ɪnts]    [ants]

Pronounce the following words.

| | | |
|---|---|---|
| [sənz] | [lísənd] | [bɪgɪnz] |
| [spunz] | [téləfond] | [gardənz] |
| [faɪndz][2] | [kwésčənd] | [kwɛsčənz] |
| [ɛndz] | [ménčənd] | [pərsənz] |
| [wants] | [stúdənts] | [rɛ́strənts] |
| [kaunts] | [pɛ́rənts] | [dífrəns] |
| [sɛnts] | [dɪpartmənts] | [əpartmənts] |

Practice the following sentences.

---

[1]Note to the teacher: **For** an explanation of the use of this exercise see the introduction to this volume.

[2]Note to the teacher: It is not necessary to differentiate between [nz] and [ndz]. Acoustically they are very similar. They are differentiated here to show the simple underlying form of the word. Thus [faɪndz] represents the word FINDS and [faɪnz] would represent FINES.

[hi bɪgɪnz tə æsk kwɛsčənz]

[ðə ˈtičər tɛləfond ðə studənt]

[ðə studənts lɪsənd tə ðə tičər]

[hi wants ə nu əpartmənt]

[ðe əndərstænd ðɪ ɛksplənešənz]

Practice the following pair of sentences.

[ðə studənt əndərstændz ðə lɛsənz]

[ðə studənts əndərstænd ðə lɛsən]

## 3. Consonant clusters with [ŋ]

In the pronunciation of [ŋ] the back of the tongue touches the velum. Practice the difference between [n] and [ŋ] in the following words.

| | | | | |
|---|---|---|---|---|
| [Θɪn] | [Θɪnz] | [Θɪŋ] | [Θɪŋz] | [Θɪŋks] |
| [tæn] | [tænz] | [tæŋ] | [tæŋz] | [tæŋks] |
| [sɪn] | [sɪnz] | [sɪŋ] | [sɪŋz] | [sɪŋks] |

Pronounce the following syllables.

[ɪŋz]           [æŋz]          [ɪŋks]          [æŋks]

Practice the following.

| | | |
|---|---|---|
| [drɪŋks] | [hæŋz] | [Θæŋks] |
| [sɪŋks] | [sɪŋz] | [bæŋks] |
| [Θɪŋks] | [brɪŋz] | [tæŋks] |

[hi sɪŋz mɛni sɔŋz]

[ðə daktər Θɪŋks ðə mɛdɪsɪnz ar gʊd]

[hiz brɪŋɪŋ mɛni Θɪŋz]

[ðɛr ar mɛni bæŋks ɪn ðə sɪti]

[kold drɪŋks ar vɛri gʊd]

Memorize the following conversation.

Student C.  [dɪd yə laɪk ðə progræm]

Student D.  [yɛs aɪ ɛspɛšəli laɪkt ðə dɪfrənt sɔŋz]

## 4. Exercise in marking pauses

Mark the following paragraphs for acceptable rhythm as the first sentence is marked. Read the paragraphs after you mark them.

There is a public library/ in almost every American community./ Even small communities have public libraries where people can borrow books and use them at home without paying. There are only two requirements for a person who takes books home from a public library: he must be a resident of the community (or a student at the university) which owns the library, and he must obey the library rules.

The most important rule of every library is that books must be returned on the date when they are due. This date is written on a card at the back of the book. A person who returns a book after the date on which it is due has to pay a fine. He has to pay a few cents for every day that the book is overdue.

5. Practice on the reduced forms of COULD HAVE, SHOULD HAVE, MIGHT HAVE , WOULD HAVE.

Pronounce the following sentences.

[aɪ kʊd əv ˈgɔn tə ðə ˈmuvi]

[aɪ šʊd əv gɔn tə ðə muvi]

[aɪ maɪt əv gɔn tə ðə muvi]

[aɪ wʊd əv gɔn tə ðə muvi]

Notice the reduced forms of COULD HAVE, SHOULD HAVE, MIGHT HAVE, WOULD HAVE.

|             | Full Form    | Reduced Form |
|-------------|--------------|--------------|
| could have  | [kʊd hæv]    | [kʊd əv]     |
| should have | [šʊd hæv]    | [šʊd əv]     |
| might have  | [maɪt hæv]   | [maɪt əv]    |
| would have  | [wʊd hæv]    | [wʊd əv]     |

a) Practice the following sentences using the reduced forms of the words.

I could have gone to the movie.

> played tennis.
> gone to the concert.
> done my assignment.
> taken a walk.
> talked to my friends.
> called up my friend.
> gone to my class.
> talked to the girl.
> gone to the dance.
> written a letter.

b) Substitute the phrases from section (a) in the following sentences. Use the reduced forms.

I should have _____.

I might have _____.

I would have _____.

## PRONUNCIATION

1. Consonant clusters with [s]
2. Consonant clusters with [š], [č], and [ǰ]
3. Exercise in marking pauses
4. Review of [e], [ɛ], and [æ]

### Review

a) Pronounce the following sentences.

1. The programs are important.
2. The customs of many lands are different.
3. The names seem difficult.
4. They understand the explanations.
5. The students listened to their teacher.
6. The teacher telephoned the student.
7. The students understand the lesson.
8. He's bringing many things.
9. The doctor thinks the medicines are good.
10. He sings many songs.

b) Practice the following conversation from memory.

Student C. Did you like the program.
Student D. Yes, I especially liked the different songs.

c) Pronounce the following sentences using the reduced forms of COULD HAVE, SHOULD HAVE, MIGHT HAVE, WOULD HAVE.

1. He could have called up his friend.
2. They should have written a letter.
3. She might have talked to the girl.
4. I would have gone to my class.
5. He could have taken a walk.
6. They would have gone to the concert.
7. We might have played tennis.
8. He should have gone to his class.

### 1. Consonant clusters with [s]

The sound [s] is pronounced very clearly in English. Pronounce the following syllables and words.

| [ssstə] | [ssspə] | [ssskə] | [ssslə] | [sssmə] | [ssswə] |
|---------|---------|---------|---------|---------|---------|
| [stə]   | [spə]   | [skə]   | [slə]   | [smə]   | [swə]   |

| [st] | [sp] | [sk] | [sl] |
|------|------|------|------|
| [stæmp] | [spik] | [skul] | [slip] |
| [stɔr] | [spɛnd] | [sket] | [slo] |
| [stap] | [spun] | | |
| [stɛrz] | [spič] | [sm] | [sw] |
| [stænd] | [spok] | | |
| [stúdənt] | [spǽnɪš] | [smok] | [swɪm] |
| [stǽndərd] | [spélɪŋ] | [smaɪl] | [swit] |

154

Practice the following sentences. Pronounce the [s] sound very clearly.

[ðə ˈstudənts ar ˈstədiɪŋ]

[ðə ˈstɔr ɪz an ˈmen strit]

[hi spiks ˈsloli]

[hi smoks ə ˈpàɪp]

[ši yužuəli ˈsmaɪlz]

[pliz stap ðə ˈkar]

[ðɛr ˈslipɪŋ naʊ]

The sound [s] at the ends of words is also pronounced very clearly. Pronounce the following syllables.

| [ɪsk] | [æsk] | [ɪst] | [ost] | [eks] | [æks] |
| [ɪsks] | [æsks] | [ɪsts] | [osts] | [əsts] | [ɛkst] |

Pronounce the following.

| [æsk] | [list] | [dɛsks] |
| [dɛsk] | [ĵəst] | [lʊks] |
| [læst] | [most] | [smoks] |
| [pæst] | [fərst] | [nɛkst] |

The teacher will pronounce the following pairs of words. Pronounce them.

| [lɪsts] | [lɪss] |
| [kɔsts] | [kɔss] |
| [gɛsts] | [gɛss] |
| [læsts] | [læss] |

In ordinary conversation the combination [sts] at the end of a word often becomes a long [s].

Practice the following sentences.

[hi ˈæsks ˈmɛni ˈkwɛsčənz]

[ðə ˈlɪst ɪz vɛri ˈlɔŋ]

[ðɛr ar tu ˈdɛsks ɪn ðə ˈrum]

[ðə fərst ˈkwɛsčən ɪz vɛri ˈdɪfɪkəlt]

[ðə kansərt ˈlæsts əntɪl tɛn əˈklàk]

[hi ɔfən ˈtɔks tə ˈĵan]

[hi lʊks ˈtàɪrd]

[hi ˈteks tu ˈkɔrˌsɪz]

Practice the difference between the following sentences. Use either [-sts] or [s---] in the word GUESTS.

The guest eats dinner.

The guests eat dinner.

Memorize the following conversation.

Teacher A. [hwɛr̩ ar ðə lɪsts əv studənts]

Teacher B. [ðə læst lɪst ɪz an ðə dɛsk]

## 2. Consonant clusters with [š], [č], and [ǰ]

Notice the difference in pronunciation between [š], [č] and [ǰ] in the following words. Pronounce them.

| [šo] | [šip] | [šæm] | [čap] |
|------|-------|-------|-------|
| [čo] | [čip] | [ǰæm] | [ǰuz] |
| [ǰo] | [ǰip] | [šap] | [čuz] |

Pronounce the following syllables.

[əšt]    [əčt]    [əǰd]    [ošt]    [očt]    [oǰd]

Practice the difference between the following.

[wɔšt]  washed                                    [wačt]  watched

[ðə məðər wɔšt ðə bebi]

[ðə məðər wačt ðə bebi]

Pronounce the following.

| [kæšt] | [wačt] | [eǰd] |
|--------|--------|-------|
| [pušt] | [strɛčt] | [keǰd] |
| [wɔšt] | [skræčt] | [čenǰd] |
| [brəšt] | [mæčt] | [ərénǰd] |

[ðe čenǰd ðɛr plænz]

[ši wɔšt ənd brəšt ər hɛr]

[ðə kæt skræčt ðə bɔɪ]

[ðə bɔɪz wačt ðə besbɔl gem]

[ðe ərenǰd ðə fərnɪčər ɪn ðə rum]

Memorize the following conversation.

Dentist A. [hwət dɪd ši du]

Dentist B. [ši wɔšt ðə bebi]

Substitute [wačt] for [wɔšt] in the preceding conversation and practice it.

## 3. Exercise in marking pauses

Indicate the pauses in the following paragraphs as in the first sentence.

I am a doctor of pediatrics/ in Colombia/ where I have been a clinical advisor/ in the emergency hospital/ for five years./ I hope to attend a university in the United States during the year in order to take advanced courses in pediatrics.

Will you please give me information about advanced courses in medicine at the university? I would also appreciate information concerning entrance requirements, fees, and the registration dates for the fall semester.

4. Review of [e], [ɛ], and [æ]

Practice the following words. Make a clear distinction between [e], [ɛ], and [æ].

| [men] | [sɛd] | [bǽtəl] | [kǽptən] |
| [lɛt] | [hæd] | [sɛ́ldəm] | [lɛ́tər] |
| [kæn] | [nem] | [létər] | [féməs] |

Memorize the following conversation.

Student: [huz ðæt mæn]

Teacher: [hiz ə feməs dɛntɪst]

## PRONUNCIATION

1. Consonant clusters with [t] and [d]
2. 2-4-3 intonation curve in combinations of sentences
3. Rhythm drill
4. Review of [ə] and [a]

Review

a) Pronounce the following sentences.

1. The students are studying the lessons.
2. The store is on State Street.
3. He speaks slowly.
4. Please stop at the next street.
5. The first question is interesting.
6. He's taking two courses.
7. He often talks to his teachers.
8. They arranged the books on the desk.

b) Practice the following conversation from memory.

Dentist A.  What did she do?
Dentist B.  She washed ( watched) the baby.

c) Practice the following conversation from memory. Which word or words contain the sound [e]? the sound [ɛ]? the sound [æ]?

Student:  Who's that man?
Teacher:  He's a famous dentist.

1. Consonant clusters with [t] and [d]

The sounds [t] and [d] are pronounced with the tongue on the tooth ridge. Pull your tongue back so that it does not touch the teeth and pronounce the following syllables.

| | | | | |
|---|---|---|---|---|
| [əst] | [əšt] | [əkt] | [əpt] | [əft] |
| [əvd] | [əbd] | [əzd] | [əmd] | [əld] |
| [ənd] | [ərd] | [əǰd] | [ənǰd] | [əčt] |

Pronounce the following.

| [st] | [št] | [kt] | [pt] |
|---|---|---|---|
| embraced | cashed | walked | stopped |
| discussed | washed | locked | helped |
| decreased | brushed | looked | slept |
| impressed | clashed | picked | hoped |

| [ft] | [ld] | [zd] | [vd] |
|---|---|---|---|
| left | called | caused | lived |
| laughed | cold | closed | arrived |
| coughed | smiled | supposed | believed |

| [nd] | [md] | [rd] | [ǰd] |
|---|---|---|---|
| listened | seemed | preferred | changed |
| learned | combed | prepared | arranged |
| mentioned | climbed | ordered | judged |

158

|                        |                        |
|------------------------|------------------------|
| They passed it.        | They called it.        |
| They cashed it.        | They closed it.        |
| They locked it.        | They believed it.      |
| They stopped it.       | They learned it.       |
| They left it.          | They climbed it.       |
| They preferred it.     | They changed it.       |
| They ordered it.       | They mentioned it.     |

Practice the following sentences. Pay particular attention to the pronunciation of [t] and [d] in combinations with other consonants.

1. The teacher smiled at the class.
2. The man stopped and helped the boy.
3. They closed all of the doors and windows.
4. All of the students told stories.
5. They described their activities at the university.
6. He advised me to go to the dentist.
7. They remembered all of the answers.
8. He lived in New York for ten years.
9. She walked down the street.
10. He combed his hair.

Memorize the following conversations. Supply the appropriate month.

Teacher:   [hwɛn dɪd yə əraɪv ɪn ðɪs kəntri]

Student:   [aɪ əraɪvd ɪn - - - -]

Teacher:   [hwɛn dɪd yə liv yər kəntri]

Student:   [aɪ lɛft ɪn - - - -]

Student C.  [hwət dɪd yə du bɪfɔr yə kem tə klæs]

Student D.  [aɪ wɔšt maɪ fés bɾəšt maɪ tiθ ənd komd maɪ hɛr]

## 2. 2-4-3 intonation curve in combinations of sentences

The instructor will read the following sentences; notice the 2-4-3 intonation curve at the end of the first part of the sentence. Pronounce the sentences.

When you meet him, tell him what I said.

I don't know, but I'm going to find out.

We can go to the theater, or we can go to a dance.

Pronounce the following sentences slowly. Use the 2-4-3 intonation curve in the first part of the sentence.

1. John wasn't a good student, but he studied carefully.
2. I didn't go, but I wish I had.
3. I want to go to the movie, but I don't have any time.
4. After the class was over, we went to the dance.
5. You must attend class regularly, or you're not going to learn anything.

3. <u>Rhythm drill</u>

Read the following sentences smoothly with the intonation as marked.

1. [ǰan ǝnd ǰɪm ǝr stuḋǝnts ǝt ðǝ yunɪvǝrsɪti]
2. [ǰan ɪz tɔlǝr ðǝn ǰɪm]
3. [bǝt ǰɪm ɪz mɔr ɪntrɪstɪŋ ðǝn ǰan]
4. [ðe go tǝ ðǝ sem klæsɪz]
5. [ðe lɪv ɪn ðǝ sem haʊs]
6. [ðe ɔfǝn it ǝt ðǝ sem rɛstrǝnt]
7. [ǰɪm dǝzǝnt stǝdi ǝz mǝč ǝz ǰan]
8. [ǰan ɪz ǝ bɛtǝr stuḋǝnt ðǝn ǰɪm]
9. [ǰan ǝnd ǰɪm ǝr faɪn bɔɪz ǝnd ðe ǝr yužuǝli vɛri plɛzǝnt]

Read the following paragraph with appropriate rhythm and intonation. If your teacher tells you the intonation is incorrect look at the preceding sentences and repeat them.

John and Jim are students at the university. John is taller than Jim. But Jim is more interesting than John. They go to the same classes. They live in the same house. They often eat at the same restaurant. Jim doesn't study as much as John. John is a better student than Jim. John and Jim are fine boys, and they are usually very pleasant.

4. <u>Review of [ǝ] and [a]</u>

Practice the difference between [ǝ] and [a] in the following.

| [kǝt] | [sǝmtaɪmz] | [nat] | [faðǝr] |
| [hat] | [bátǝl] | [ǝðǝr] | [máðǝr] |
| [sǝm] | [bǝtǝr] | [kǝzɪn] | [brǝðǝr] |
| [ǰǝst] | [hǝŋgri] | [lǝnč] | [bɪkɔ́z] |

Memorize the following conversation. Pay particular attention to the sounds [ǝ] and [a].

Lawyer A.      [ar yǝ hǝŋgri]

Lawyer B.      [no aɪm nat aɪ ǰǝst fɪnɪšt maɪ lǝnč]

# LESSON XXVI

## PRONUNCIATION

1. Consonant clusters with [l]
2. Spelling aids to pronunciation
3. Review of [u] and [ʊ]

Review

a) Pronounce the following words.

| | | |
|---|---|---|
| cashed | left | brushed |
| looked | caused | laughed |
| stopped | lived | arranged |
| discussed | ordered | mentioned |

b) Pronounce the following sentences.

1. John washed and shaved.
2. They walked and talked for an hour.
3. I stopped and locked the door.
4. They expressed their opinions.
5. We received many letters yesterday.
6. He smiled when I told him the story.
7. John noticed the boy in the hall.
8. We helped him with his lessons.

c) Practice the following conversation from memory.

Student C.  What did you do before you came to class?
Student D.  I washed my face, brushed my teeth, and combed my hair.

d) Practice the following conversation from memory. Which word or words contain the sound [ə]? the sound [a]?

Lawyer A.  Are you hungry?
Lawyer B.  No, I'm not. I just finished my lunch.

## 1. Consonant clusters with [l]

Practice the following syllables.

[plə]     [blə]     [klə]     [glə]     [slə]     [flə]

Pronounce the following words and sentences.

| [pl] | [bl] | [kl] | [gl] |
|---|---|---|---|
| plate | blade | close | glass |
| play | blouse | class | Gloria |
| plan | block | clap | glide |
| plant | black | closet | glad |

| [sl] | [fl] |
|---|---|
| slip | fly |
| asleep | flower |
| slide | flavor |
| sleep | flag |

161

1. The blouse is black.
2. He slipped on the floor.
3. The whole class was sleepy.
4. The flag is flying over the building.
5. She likes plants and flowers.
6. The closet is very large.

Memorize the following conversation.

Student A.    [pliz│kloz│ðə klazıt│dɔr]

Student B.    [aı│kænt ðɛr ər tu mɛni│Θıŋz an ðə│flɔr]

Practice the following syllables.

   [ɛlp]        [əlt]        [ılk]        [old]        [əlz]        [ərl]

Pronounce the following words and sentences.

| helped | boiled | smiled | tells |
| felt | sold | controlled | bills |
| difficult | cold | rolled | feels |
| milk | old | called | pills |

| | bottles | hospitals | |
| | pencils | articles | |
| | examples | girls | |
| | controls | battles | |

1. He felt cold.
2. He's ten years old.
3. The girl smiled and called to him.
4. She boiled the milk.
5. There are several bottles on the tables.
6. The examples are difficult.
7. The pencils are old.
8. They gave you many pills in the hospital.

Memorize the following conversations.

John.    [aı dont əndərstænd│ðiz ɛgzæmpləz]

Robert.    [æsk ðæt│gərl ši kən│hɛlp│yu]

## 2. Spelling aids to pronunciation

English words are often not pronounced as they are spelled. There are many regularities in spelling, however, which will help you to pronounce new words. The following list shows you some of these regularities.[1]

---

[1] Note to the teacher: It should be emphasized that these are not RULES, since there are many exceptions to these general statements.

| Examples | Sound | Spelling Formula (C represents any consonant) |
|---|---|---|
| a. cat<br>map<br>ask<br>last | [æ] | a + C (C) |
| bed<br>desk<br>left<br>men | [ɛ] | e + C (C) |
| clerk[1]<br>term | [ər] | er + (C) |
| big<br>list<br>pin<br>bill | [ɪ] | i + C (C) |
| bird[1]<br>flirt<br>dirt | [ər] | ir + (C) |
| not<br>clock<br>hot<br>sock | [a] | o + C (C) |
| word[1]<br>work<br>worm | [ər] | or + (C) |
| but<br>luck<br>cut<br>rung | [ə] | u + C (C) |
| turn[1]<br>burn<br>curl | [ər] | ur + (C) |
| b. take<br>made<br>lake<br>late | [e] | a + C + e (Final e in this formula is not pronounced) |

---

[1] Note to the teacher: The combination of vowel + r is an exception to the regular statement of vowel and consonant combinations.

| | | |
|---|---|---|
| nine<br>five<br>dime<br>pipe | [aɪ] | i̱ + C + e̤ |
| note<br>bone<br>coke<br>phone | [o] | o̱ + C + e |
| tube<br>rude<br>rule<br>tune | [u] | u̱ + C + e |

c. three<br>   tree<br>    sleep<br>   need     [i]     <u>ee</u>

| | | |
|---|---|---|
| three<br>tree<br>sleep<br>need | [i] | ee |
| true<br>blue<br>due | [u] | ue |
| boat<br>soap<br>coal | [o] | oa |
| out<br>mouth<br>sound | [aʊ] | ou |
| law<br>saw<br>lawn | [ɔ] | aw |

d. table<br>   vegetable<br>   gentle<br>   able     [əl]     C + le (in un-<br>stressed syllables)

| | | |
|---|---|---|
| familiar<br>popular | [ər] | ar, er, or (in<br>unstressed syllables) |
| teacher<br>water | [ər] | |
| error<br>elevator | [ər] | |

Pronounce the following.

| sand | not | pot | invitation | table |
|------|-----|-----|-----------|-------|
| cot | bun | crab | nut | able |
| hut | dollar | clock | cap | understandable |
| map | lamp | but | drove | vegetable |

1. I like crab salad.
2. The lamp is worth five dollars.
3. She has a lot of bottles.
4. This coke is hot.
5. I work from eight o'clock to five o'clock.
6. This is the list.
7. He sleeps late.
8. He ate lunch and supper with us.
9. He dropped the rock on the box.
10. The bus is stuck in the mud.

Dr. White got up late this morning. It was seven thirty so he had to rush. His wife got breakfast and he ate rapidly. Then he ran to class. He said, "As a rule I'm on time, but today my clock didn't work."

3. Review of [u] and [ʊ]

Pronounce the following. Make a clear distinction between [u] and [ʊ].

| | | |
|---|---|---|
| [pul] | [æftərnún] | [grup] |
| [tʊk] | [šúgər] | [gʊd] |
| [šʊd] | [ǽtɪtud] | [sut] |
| [kul] | [wʊl] | [byútɪful] |

[hi tʊk ɪt]

[ðə sut ɪz med əv wʊl]

[ðɪs grup šʊd stədi]

[šiz ə byutɪful wʊmən]

Memorize the following conversation.

Alfred.  [aɪ hæv ə nu sut]

Bill.    [ɪz ɪt wʊl]

Alfred.  [yɛs ɪt ɪz]

## PRONUNCIATION

1. Consonant clusters and combinations with [Ө] and [ð]
2. Exercise in marking pauses
3. Review of [o] and [ɔ]

Review

a) Practice the following conversations from memory.

Student A. Please close the closet door.
Student B. I can't. There are too many things on the floor.

John. I don't understand these examples.
Robert. Ask that girl. She can help you.

b) Practice the following conversation. Which word or words contain the sound [u]? the sound [ʊ] ?

Alfred. I have a new suit.
Bill. Is it wool?
Alfred. Yes, it is.

c) Pronounce the following sentences. Notice the regularities in spelling which help you to pronounce the words accurately.

1. The new term begins in two weeks.
2. The bills are due now.
3. The clock is not working.
4. These vegetables taste very good.
5. The tuition is not expensive.
6. The ten cent store is also called the five and dime.
7. The children made boats out of soap.
8. They asked about the rules.
9. The clerk is selling many things today.
10. He sang a popular tune.

1. Consonant clusters and combinations with [Ө] and [ð]

| [ɪfӨ] | [ɛlfӨ] | [ɛnӨ] | [etӨ] | [ɛpӨ] |
|-------|--------|-------|-------|-------|
| fifth | tenth | eighth | | ninth |
| twelfth | month | month | | eleventh |

Many combinations of consonants occur in English within phrases. Pronounce the following combinations in successive syllables.

| [ɪks-Өə] | [ip-Өə] | [ən-Өə] | [af-Өə] |
|----------|---------|---------|---------|
| keep thinking | enough things | one thing | six things |
| keep thanking | enough thanks | one theater | six theaters |

Pronounce the following sentences several times. Be sure to pronounce [Ө] accurately.

1. They keep thinking about it.
2. There are enough things to do.
3. There is one theater in the town.

4. He had six thing to remember.
5. They keep thanking me for the gift.

Pronounce the following combinations several times.

    [əs-Өə]    [əs-ðə]    [əz-ðə]    [əš-ðə]    [əč-ðə]

Practice the following phrases and sentences. When you pronounce [s] or [z] keep your teeth closed. When you pronounce [Ө] and [ð] put your tongue between your teeth.

| [s-Ө] | [s-ð] | [z-Ө] |
|---|---|---|
| stops thinking | what's this | those things |
| keeps thinking | what's that | these thoughts |
| keeps things | it's there | he's thirsty |

| [z-ð] | [š-ð] | [č-ð] |
|---|---|---|
| he's the man | cash that check | watch the child |
| where's the house | wash the car | watch the class |
| who's the man | wash the window | touch the glass |

1. What's this on the table?
2. He's going to wash the car.
3. He's the man that came yesterday.
4. She keeps things in the closet.
5. Those things are very important.

Memorize the following conversations.

Doctor X.    [hwəts ˈðæt]

Doctor Y.    [ɪts ðə ˈbʊk aɪ bɔt ˈyɛstərde]

Gloria.    [hwət wəz ruӨ ˈӨɪŋkɪŋ əbaut]

Mary.    [ši wəz ˈӨɪŋkɪŋ əbaut ðə ˈmuvi]

## 2. Exercise in marking pauses

Indicate the pauses in the following paragraphs as in the first sentence. Read the paragraphs with smooth sentence rhythm.

Students from other countries/ often ask questions/ concerning university classes/ in the United States./ There are usually four kinds of classes in American universities. First, many subjects are taught in LECTURE courses. Lecture classes are often large. The professor speaks from notes or from a written lecture concerning the subject of the course. Lecture courses are valuable because the professors who teach them are specialists in their fields, and students who take accurate notes of a lecture profit by the experience and knowledge of the lecturer.

The second kind of university class is the RECITATION class. Recitation classes can be divided into two groups. When recitation classes are held in addition to lecture classes during the same course, the class is called a QUIZ SECTION. The second kind of recitation class is not combined with a lecture class. In such classes, the instructor talks informally and asks questions. The students can also ask questions. Recitation classes are usually rather small, so that each student can have an opportunity to participate in the discussion.

The fist two kinds of university classes are for both elementary and advanced students. However, the third kind of class, the SEMINAR CLASS, is for advanced students only.

The seminar class meets in a room which contains a large table. The students and the professor sit around the table and discuss special problems which pertain to the subject of the course. In a seminar class, the students prepare reports upon their own research and read these reports to the rest of the class.

The fourth kind of university class is the LABORATORY class. Laboratory classes are especially important in technical and scientific courses. A laboratory section often meets for three or four hours for experiments and technical research.

3. Review of [o] and [ɔ]

Pronounce the following. Make a clear distinction between [o] and [ɔ].

| [bɔt] | [sɔŋ] | [tɔr] |
|-------|-------|-------|
| [kot] | [kɔst] | [wɔrn] |
| [dont] | [tost] | [ʃok] |
| [kɔfi] | [sop] | [roz] |

[ðə sop wəz ɪkspɛnsɪv]

[ɪt kɔst ə lat]

[ðə kɔfi ɪz rɛdi]

[ðe bɔt mɛni θɪŋz]

Memorize the following conversation.

Lawyer K.    [du yə no ðɪs sɔŋ]

Lawyer L.    [no aɪ dont]

# LESSON XXVIII

## PRONUNCIATION

1. Intonation of attached questions
2. Mastery exercise (first half)

### Review

a) Practice the following sentences. Pronounce the combinations of consonants accurately.

1. We locked the door before we left.
2. Did you believe his story?
3. They listened to the music.
4. Who's the man next to your friend?
5. We arrived before the concert began.
6. Please don't touch the dog.
7. He's thirsty now.
8. I'm going to New York next month.
9. He lives on the fifth floor.
10. He's going to wash the car this afternoon.

b) Pronounce the following questions. Use the 2-4 intonation.

1. Is he here?
2. What is it?
3. Can you come?
4. Do you know him?
5. Is it cold today?
6. Where are you?
7. When are you coming?
8. Are they busy?
9. Is he a dentist?
10. Are you going?

## 1. Intonation of attached questions

Pronounce the following sentence in imitation of the teacher.

He's a ⌐doctor, isn't he?

Notice the 2-4 intonation at the end of the sentence. We are saying, "I KNOW he is a doctor. I am only asking you to confirm what I have said. I am making conversation."

Pronounce the following sentence in imitation of the teacher.

He's a ⌐doctor, isn't he?

Notice the 3-2 intonation at the end of the sentence. We are saying, "I really don't know whether he is a doctor or not. I'm asking you for information."

The 2-4 intonation curve on questions like these usually indicates that the speaker is not asking for information. The 3-2 intonation curve on questions like this usually indicates that the speaker is asking for information.

Practice the following sentences with the intonation as marked.

169

He's a doctor, isn't he?      She's a doctor, isn't she?

|  |  |
|---|---|
| dentist | dentist |
| lawyer | lawyer |
| engineer | engineer |
| professor | professor |
| teacher | teacher |

He isn't a doctor, is he?      She isn't a doctor, is she?

|  |  |
|---|---|
| dentist | dentist |
| lawyer | lawyer |
| engineer | engineer |
| professor | professor |
| teacher | teacher |

It's hot today, isn't it?      It isn't hot today, is it?

|  |  |
|---|---|
| nice | nice |
| rainy | rainy |
| cloudy | cloudy |
| cold | cold |
| cool | cool |

Practice the following sentences with the intonation as marked. We are asking for information.

He isn't a doctor, is he?      It's hot today, isn't it?

|  |  |
|---|---|
| dentist | nice |
| lawyer | rainy |
| teacher | cloudy |
| professor | cold |
| engineer | cool |

Supply the last part of the following sentences. Use the 2-4 intonation curve.

Example:    She's a nurse, _____ ?

She's a nurse, isn't she?

1. He's a teacher, _____ ?
2. They're engineers, _____ ?
3. He's a doctor, _____ ?
4. It's cold today, _____ ?
5. It's an interesting book, _____ ?
6. They're good students, _____ ?
7. It's a long trip, _____ ?
8. The professors are early, _____ ?
9. She's going to Detroit tomorrow, _____ ?
10. John's late today, _____ ?

Supply the last part of the following sentences. Use the 3-2 intonation curve.

Example:    She's a nurse, _____ ?

She's a nurse, isn't she?

1. He's a teacher, _____ ?
2. They're engineers, _____ ?
3. He's a doctor, _____ ?
4. It's cold today, _____ ?
5. It's an interesting book, _____ ?
6. They're good students, _____ ?
7. It's a long trip, _____ ?
8. The professors are early, _____ ?
9. She's going to Detroit tomorrow, _____ ?
10. John's late today, _____ ?

2. Mastery exercise (first half)[1]

Practice the following paragraphs. Mark the sentences for pauses. Pay particular attention to the accurate pronunciation of the vowel sounds and [r].

### Mastery Exercise

This exercise contains a variety of difficulties in English. We should practice these words until we can say them just like a native speaker of English.

Student A. Is it good to practice them?

Student B. Yes, I think so.

Student A. Then, how does it help me?

Student B. Many people think that a foreign accent is caused by thousands of various little errors.

Student A. But this isn't so, is it?

Student B. No. Linguistic science has proved that when we learn a foreign language we make only a small number of errors, but we repeat these same errors many times.

---

[1] Note to the teacher: This exercise is provided to give the students practice on the production of accurate sounds, intonation, and rhythm. It has been divided into two parts for ease of presentation. The second half will be found in Lesson XXIX.

# LESSON XXIX

## PRONUNCIATION

1. Variations in pronunciation in the United States
2. Mastery exercise (second half)

Review

a) Pronounce the following sentences.

1. We discussed the lesson.
2. She brushed her hair.
3. He looked at it.
4. They stopped the car.
5. He laughed at the boy.
6. She smiled at him.
7. I closed the door.
8. They arrived yesterday.
9. The boy seemed tired.
10. We ordered the books.
11. The girl changed her mind.
12. The student learned the words.
13. They passed the store.
14. He cashed his check.
15. I slept late today.

b) Pronounce the following sentences. Pay particular attention to the combinations of consonants.

1. The examples seemed easy.
2. Where's the man you told me about.
3. Those things are very important.
4. There were six things on the table.
5. He feels very well today.
6. She was thinking about her sister.
7. She put a lot of bottles on the table.
8. Please watch the blackboard.

1. Variations in pronunciation in the United States

The pronunciation of English among speakers in the United States is not, of course, uniform. There are many differences in pronunciation in different parts of the United States. There are many differences in the pronunciation of the same words even in the speech of one person. This discussion will indicate only a few of the differences that you will hear in the pronunciation of the words presented in this book.

There are several different pronunciations of unstressed vowels. In this book the pronunciation of unstressed vowels in certain words has been given as the writer pronounced them.

Many individual differences in pronunciation are not specifically limited to geographical areas. Notice the differences in the following words.

a) Alternation of [ɪ] and [ɛ] in unstressed syllables

| | | |
|---|---|---|
| expensive | [ɪkspénsɪv] | [ɛkspénsɪv] |
| extend | [ɪksténd] | [ɛksténd] |

|           |              |              |
|-----------|--------------|--------------|
| external  | [ɪkstə́rnəl]  | [ɛkstə́rnəl]  |
| explain   | [ɪksplén]    | [ɛksplén]    |
| excuse    | [ɪkskyúz]    | [ɛkskyúz]    |
| express   | [ɪksprέs]    | [ɛksprέs]    |
| enjoy     | [ɪnǰóɪ]      | [ɛnǰóɪ]      |
| inquire   | [ɪnkwáɪr]    | [ɛnkwáɪr]    |
| invite    | [ɪnváɪt]     | [ɛnváɪt]     |
| perfect   | [pə́rfɪkt]    | [pə́rfɛkt]    |
| subject   | [sə́bǰɪkt]    | [sə́bǰɛkt]    |
| object    | [ábǰɪkt]     | [ábǰɛkt]     |

ε

b) <u>Alternation of [ɪ] and [ə] in unstressed syllables</u>

|             |                |                |
|-------------|----------------|----------------|
| delicious   | [dɪlíšəs]      | [dəlíšəs]      |
| department  | [dɪpártmənt]   | [dəpártmənt]   |
| describe    | [dɪskráɪb]     | [dəskráɪb]     |
| detail      | [dɪtél]        | [dətél]        |
| discouraged | [dɪskə́rɪǰd]    | [dəskə́rəǰd]    |
| begin       | [bɪgín]        | [bəgín]        |
| behave      | [bɪhév]        | [bəhév]        |
| believe     | [bɪlív]        | [bəlív]        |
| prefer      | [prɪfə́r]      | [prəfə́r]      |
| prepare     | [prɪpέr]       | [prəpέr]       |
| prescribe   | [prɪskráɪb]    | [prəskráɪb]    |
| pretend     | [prɪtέnd]      | [prətέnd]      |
| rely        | [rɪláɪ]        | [rəláɪ]        |
| require     | [rɪkwáɪr]      | [rəkwáɪr]      |
| select      | [sɪlέkt]       | [səlέkt]       |

c) <u>Alternation of [ɔ] and [a] in stressed syllables</u>

|           |           |           |
|-----------|-----------|-----------|
| long      | [laŋ]     | [lɔŋ]     |
| song      | [saŋ]     | [sɔŋ]     |
| wrong     | [raŋ]     | [rɔŋ]     |
| strong    | [straŋ]   | [strɔŋ]   |
| dog       | [dag]     | [dɔg]     |
| cloth     | [klaθ]    | [klɔθ]    |
| chocolate | [čáklət]  | [čóklət]  |
| cough     | [kaf]     | [kɔf]     |
| quality   | [kwálɪtɪ] | [kwɔ́lɪtɪ]|
| quantity  | [kwántɪtɪ]| [kwɔ́ntɪtɪ]|
| wash      | [waš]     | [wɔš]     |
| want      | [want]    | [wɔnt]    |
| on        | [an]      | [ɔn]      |
| office    | [áfɪs]    | [ófɪs]    |
| often     | [áfən]    | [ófən]    |
| Oregon    | [árɪgən]  | [órɪgən]  |
| borrow    | [báro]    | [bóro]    |
| sorry     | [sári]    | [sóri]    |

d) Alternation of [u] and [yu] in stressed syllables

| | | |
|---|---|---|
| new | [nu] | [nyu] |
| news | [nuz] | [nyus] |
| student | [stúdənt] | [styúdənt] |
| overdue | [ovərdú] | [ovərdyú] |
| introduce | [ɪntrədús] | [ɪntrədyús] |
| produce | [prədús] | [prədyus] |

You will also hear some of the following differences in pronunciation in the pronunci-stion of people from different parts of the United States. The following differences are mainly limited to certain geographical areas.

e) [æ] and [a] in words like ask, glass

| | | |
|---|---|---|
| ask | [æsk] | [ask][1] |
| bath | [bæΘ] | [baΘ] |
| class | [klæs] | [klas] |
| dance | [dæns] | [dans] |
| example | [ɛgzæmpəl] | [ɛgzampəl] |
| glass | [glæs] | [glas] |
| half | [hæf] | [haf] |
| laugh | [læf] | [laf] |
| last | [læst] | [last] |
| path | [pæΘ] | [paΘ] |
| past | [pæst] | [past] |
| pass | [pæs] | [pas] |

f) [r] after an unstressed vowel in words like father, teacher

| | | |
|---|---|---|
| doctor | [dáktər] | [dáktə] |
| father | [fáðər] | [fáðə] |
| mother | [məðər] | [məðə] |
| sister | [sɪstər] | [sɪstə] |
| farmer | [fármər] | [fámə] |
| order | [ɔrdər] | [ɔdə] |
| teacher | [tíčər] | [tíčə] |
| speaker | [spíkər] | [spíkə] |
| smoker | [smókər] | [smókə] |
| waiter | [wétər] | [wétə] |
| water | [wɔtər] | [wɔtə] |
| letter | [lɛtər] | [lɛtə] |
| singer | [síŋər] | [síŋə] |
| sugar | [šúgər] | [šúgə] |

g) [r] after a stressed vowel in words like farm, girl[2]

| | | |
|---|---|---|
| fork | [fɔrk] | [fɔk] |

---

[1] The pronunciation given in this column is frequently heard in eastern New England and the south-eastern part of the United States.

[2] Notice that the difference in pronunciation occurs in words spelled with r and followed by a consonant.

| farm | [farm] | [fam] |
|------|--------|-------|
| girl | [gərl] | [gəl] |
| quart | [kwɔrt] | [kwɔt] |
| yard | [yard] | [yad] |
| barn | [barn] | [ban] |
| sharp | [šarp] | [šap] |
| perfect | [pə́rfɪkt] | [pə́fɪkt] |
| sermon | [sə́rmən] | [sə́mən] |
| barber | [bárbər] | [bábə] |
| research | [rɪsə́rč] | [rɪsə́č] |
| entertainment | [ɛntərté̇nmənt] | [ɛntəté̇nmənt] |
| garden | [gárdən] | [gádən] |

h) [r] after a stressed vowel in words like poor, clear[1]

| door | [dɔr] | [dɔə] |
|------|-------|-------|
| explore | [ɪksplɔ́r] | [ɪksplɔ́ə] |
| shore | [šɔr] | [šɔə] |
| floor | [flɔr] | [flɔə] |
| more | [mɔr] | [mɔə] |
| clear | [klɪr] | [klɪə] |
| dear | [dɪr] | [dɪə] |
| year | [yɪr] | [yɪə] |
| sincere | [sɪnsɪ́r] | [sɪnsɪ́ə] |
| poor | [pur] | [puə] |
| pure | [pyur] | [pyuə] |
| sure | [šur] | [šuə] |
| fair | [fɛr] | [fɛə] |
| pair | [pɛr] | [pɛə] |
| square | [skwɛr] | [skwɛə] |
| prepare | [prɪpɛ́r] | [prɪpɛ́ə] |

## 2. Mastery exercise (second half)[2]

Review the first part of this exercise.

This exercise contains a variety of difficulties in English. We should practice these words until we can say them just like a native speaker of English.

> Student A. Is it good to practice them?
> Student B. Yes, I think so.
> Student A. Then, how does it help me?
> Student B. Many people think that a foreign accent is caused by thousands of various little errors.
> Student A. But this isn't so, is it?

---

[1] Observe that the difference in pronunciation occurs in final stressed syllables that end in the letters r or re preceded by a vowel letter or a combination of vowel letters.

[2] Note to the teacher: The first half of this exercise was introduced in Lesson XXVIII, p. 171. The first part is repeated here for review without intonation markings, but the major emphasis should be upon the second half at this time. The entire exercise can be reviewed from this section later.

Student B.   No. Linguistic science has proved that when we learn a foreign language we make only a small number of errors, but we repeat these same errors many times.

Continue the second half of the mastery exercise.

Student A.   What does this mean to a person learning a foreign language?

Student B.   It means, for example, that when he doesn't pronounce the vowel [æ] correctly, he makes an error every time the sound is used. Thus one error is repeated many times. It also means that if a person learns this sound well, countless errors will be eliminated.

Student A.   I am sure that PRACTICING THIS EXERCISE WILL HELP ME TO ESTABLISH GOOD HABITS OF PRONUNCIATION.

# LESSON XXX

## PRONUNCIATION

1. Review of vowels and consonants
2. Review of consonant clusters and combinations
3. Exercise on intonation and rhythm

## 1. Review of vowels and consonants

Pronounce the following words. Make a clear distinction between them.

| | a | b | c | d |
|---|---|---|---|---|
| 1. | live | leave | | |
| 2. | pill | pull | | |
| 3. | day | they | | |
| 4. | not | note | | |
| 5. | black | block | | |
| 6. | shook | should | | |
| 7. | smile | small | | |
| 8. | seem | same | | |
| 9. | do | two | | |
| 10. | this | these | | |
| 11. | those | chose | | |
| 12. | coat | caught | | |
| 13. | pair | poor | | |
| 14. | class | glass | | |
| 15. | half | have | | |
| 16. | food | foot | | |
| 17. | match | much | | |
| 18. | meal | mile | | |
| 19. | met | meet, meat | | |
| 20. | wall | hall | | |
| 21. | word | work | | |
| 22. | suit | soup | | |
| 23. | son | some | | |
| 24. | take | took | talk | |
| 25. | seem | same | some | |
| 26. | time | dime | them | |
| 27. | can | man | ran | |
| 28. | cold | sold | told | |
| 29. | come | came | comb | |
| 30. | hat | hot | what | |
| 31. | well | wool | whole | |
| 32. | then | than | them | |
| 33. | thing | think | sink | |
| 34. | tray | tree | three | |
| 35. | ice | eyes | yes | |
| 36. | path | pass | bath | |
| 37. | share | chair | there | |
| 38. | see | she | G | |
| 39. | song | sing | sang | |

(continued on next page)

| 40. | try | tray | true | |
| 41. | red | read | rode | ride |
| 42. | see | say | so | saw |
| 43. | feel | fall | fell | fill |
| 44. | but | bought | bit | bite |
| 45. | ate | eat | at | it |
| 46. | choose | juice | use | shoes |
| 47. | bad | bed | bath | that |
| 48. | yellow | Jello | | |
| 49. | wash | watch | | |
| 50. | shoe | chew | show | |
| 51. | church | shirts | | |
| 52. | just | used | dust | does |
| 53. | cause | jaws | | |
| 54. | sink | think | sings | thing |
| 55. | sleep | asleep | | |
| 56. | story | a story | history | his story |
| 57. | pass | path | bath | |
| 58. | through | shoe | show | throw |
| 59. | those | shoes | choose | |

2. Review of consonant clusters and combinations

Pronounce the following phrases accurately.

1. stop studying
2. insist on staying
3. step on a stone
4. passes a spoon
5. smile a lot
6. discover a stamp
7. still standing
8. speak slowly
9. just a student
10. ask a student
11. Mr. Smith is small
12. Mr. Smith smiles
13. an angry group
14. a brown dress
15. a pretty dress
16. improve a grade
17. a secret entrance
18. prefer bread
19. a hungry group
20. decrease gradually
21. a broken glass
22. a true impression
23. a surprised friend
24. blue clothes
25. a public class
26. a pleasant clerk
27. a quiet club
28. require a prescription
29. blue gloves
30. pleasant expression
31. a short word
32. part of his arm
33. a dark barn
34. return to work
35. a clerk served
36. built a shelf
37. felt cold
38. wants some bottles
39. builds barns
40. marks cards
41. learns the forms
42. begins the charts
43. counts the things
44. wants the rings
45. thinks of titles
46. keeps the parts
47. selects the facts
48. asks the guests
49. requests the facts
50. wastes the envelopes
51. helped the child
52. received the letter

53. prepared a list
54. looked alike
55. learned the terms
56. wiped the desks
57. controlled the child
58. noticed the lists
59. listened to him

60. coughed and laughed
61. arrived late
62. brushed the coat
63. served breakfast
64. watched the guests
65. arranged the date
66. changed the facts

3. Exercise on intonation and rhythm

Read the following paragraphs with normal rapid pronunciation. Observe the intonation lines.

Miss Marshall comes from Peru. Before she left Lima she worried about who to see when she arrived in the United States. The American Consul in Lima tried to help her.

"You don't need to worry," he said. "Mr. John Smith is going to meet you when you arrive, and he is going to advise you. He is going to answer all your questions. It's not very difficult. You're going to be all right. Now then, relax."

Miss Marshall did not relax, however.

She arrived at New York in June. The first man she met had red hair.

"Hello," Miss Marshall said. "Are you Mr. John Smith?"

"Yes," said the man with red hair. "I'm John L. Smith."

"Good. I didn't think it was going to be so easy. My name is Maria Marshall."

"How do you do," the man said. "I don't know you but I'm glad to meet you. I don't think I'm the man that you want. I'm sorry, but I must go." He left.

The next man Miss Marshall met wore a dark suit. Miss Marshall stopped him.

"Hello" she said. "Are you Mr. John Smith?"

"Yes. My name's John T. Smith, but I must meet my wife. I'm sorry but I can't stop to talk now. I hope that we meet again sometime." He left also.

The third man Miss Marshall met was tall and had white hair.

"I beg your pardon, but are you John Smith?" Miss Marshall was tired and a little discouraged. She spoke softly.

"Yes," The man said, "but I am probably not the right John Smith. I'm John R. Smith. There are five thousand John Smiths in the United States. I'm sorry that I can't help you."

After half an hour the correct Mr. John Smith arrived and found Miss Marshall.

"I'm sorry I caused you so much difficulty," he said; "I'm John Q. Smith. You can distinguish the Smiths by their middle names. Let's eat. You'll feel better after dinner."

# LESSON XXXI

## PRONUNCIATION

1. Drill on the recognition of sounds
2. The production of [ɪ]
3. The production of [ɛ]
4. Speed and rhythm drills
5. Dictation exercise
6. Unrehearsed talk

## 1. Drill on the recognition of sounds

The instructor will pronounce the words in the following columns in any order he chooses. Indicate by number the words he pronounces.

|   | a | b | c | d |
|---|-----|------|------|------|
| 1 | big | end | him | pen |
| 2 | beg | and | hen | pin |
| 3 | bag | aunt | hand | pan |
| 4 | begs | ends | hens | pins |

Pronounce some of the words in the preceding columns, one column at a time. The instructor will indicate the words that he hears.

## 2. The production of [ɪ]

Read the following paragraphs aloud. Which words contain the sound [ɪ]?

Jim's sister was sick on the sixteenth of July.

"Bring me a pencil," she told Jim. "I want to make a list of things you must bring me. I want you to bring me some pills, a mirror, and some cigarettes. Please pay the milk bill and get some tickets for the symphony concert tonight. Here's the money and the list."

Jim paid the milk bill which was three fifty. He bought a mirror for fifty cents, and the cigarettes cost fifteen cents. He got the pills at a drug store for thirty cents. While he was in the drug store he bought a cold drink for a nickel. The tickets for the symphony were two dollars and fifty cents.

"The cold drink was a nickel, "Jim told his sister. I needed a drink, so I added it to the list."

"The nickel is your wages," his sister said.

## 3. The production of [ɛ]

Read the following paragraphs. Which words contain the sound [ɛ]?

Helen French likes to write letters to friends. She loses so many pens that she has stopped writing letters in ink. She lost seven pens in seven days last week.

She left the first pen in a restaurant on Monday and she did not get it again. She left the second pen in a lecture class on Tuesday and she never went back to get it. She sent the third pen to a friend in an envelope, but the friend never received it. She lent the fourth pen to a guest at an entertainment but the guest never returned it. The fifth pen was an expensive pen, but Helen left it on a desk in the reference room of the library. Helen does not remember how she lost the rest of the pens.

180

She has not bought any more pens. She says they are too expensive. She writes her letters with a pencil.

## 4. Speed and rhythm drills

Read the following sentences with smooth sentence rhythm. Observe that the sentences in each group have similar sentence rhythm.

a) 1. The pén that I boúght at the stóre is expénsive.
   2. His síster was síck on the níneteenth of Júne.
   3. The stréet where I líve isn't fár from the bánk.
   4. The pílls that I háve aren't the kínd that you wánt.
   5. The mán from Brazíl came to sée you last níght.

b) 1. Do you knów where the cláss is?
   2. Will he cóme if I ásk him?
   3. Could you téll me the tíme?
   4. Can he gó to the cóncert?
   5. Did they knów I was thére?

c) 1. There's a níce cóat in the wíndow.
   2. There are three bóoks on the táble.
   3. We spent thóse hoúrs in the móvie.
   4. Can you téll Jóhn who they áre?
   5. There were fíftéen in the gróup.

d) 1. The síx éggs that I boúght were bád.
   2. The twó mén that I mét were Cúban.
   3. The fírst hóuse that I sáw was brówn.
   4. The néxt lésson that we stúdied was hárd.
   5. The lást hát that I hád was úgly.

## 5. Dictation exercise

Your teacher will dictate the following sentences at normal conversational speed.[1] Write them on a piece of paper.

1. The boy gave her a book.
2. She asked him some questions about it.
3. He answered all of them.
4. These were some of the questions.
5. What is the title?
6. Who is the author?
7. What is the story about?
8. Did you like it?
9. The boy told her the story.
10. He also told her that he likes it.

## 6. Unrehearsed talk

In order to learn about the mistakes which you are still making in pronunciation give a

---

[1]Note to the teacher. Use the reduced forms of the pronouns [ɪm, ər, ðəm] when reading these sentences. For example, [ðə bɔɪ gev ər ə bʊk].

2 minute talk on any of the following subjects without any previous preparation. Your teacher will tell you what errors in pronunciation you have made.

Suggested topics:

"My City"
"A City in the United States"
"A Trip"
"My Educational Plans"

# LESSON XXXII

## PRONUNCIATION

1. Drill on recognition of sounds
2. The production of [æ]
3. The production of [ə] and [ʊ]
4. Speed and rhythm drills
5. Spelling

## 1. Drill on the recognition of sounds

The instructor will pronounce the words in the following columns in any order he chooses. Indicate by number the words he pronounces.

|   | a | b | c | d |
|---|------|------|--------|-------|
| 1 | met  | lest | sleep  | sing  |
| 2 | mat  | last | slip   | think |
| 3 | mitt | list | asleep | sink  |
| 4 | mats | lost | a slip | thing |

Pronounce some of the words in the preceding columns, one column at a time. The instructor will indicate the words that he hears.

## 2. The production of [æ]

Read the following paragraphs aloud. Which words contain the sound [æ]?

Mr. Hanley comes from New Hampshire and Mr. Sanderson comes from Massachusetts. One Saturday afternoon they sat on the grass of the campus of the university and talked about books.

"THE YOUNG MAN OF CARACAS," Mr. Hanley said, "is a fat, blue book."

"No, it isn't," Mr. Sanderson said. "It's a narrow, black book. I read it a few weeks ago."

"I beg your pardon, but I read it also, "Mr. Hanley answered," and it was a fat blue book."

"If it's a fat blue book, I'll buy you a soda," Mr. Sanderson said.

Mr. Hanley and Mr. Sanderson crossed the campus and went into the library. They knew about the catalog and the stacks but they had never used the catalog and they had no plan of action. They examined the catalog for half an hour. They could not find the book that they wanted.

"Let's ask a librarian and see what happens," Mr. Sanderson said.

They went to the desk and asked: "Do you have THE YOUNG MAN OF CARACAS?"

"Have you examined the catalog?" the man asked.

"The catalog doesn't have it listed," Mr. Hanley said. "It's a fat, blue book."

"It's a narrow, black book," Mr. Sanderson added.

"The size doesn't matter," the man said. "Wait a minute, I'll look in the stacks."

He came back, walking rapidly.

"Here it is," he said. "It's a narrow blue book. Do you want to take it out?"

"No, thank you," Mr. Hanley said.

Mr. Hanley bought Mr. Sanderson a soda; Mr. Sanderson bought Mr. Hanley a soda. The librarian was a little angry about the matter.

Repeat aloud as much of the preceding narrative as you can remember.

3. The production of [ə] and [ʊ]

Read the following paragraphs aloud. Which words contain the sound [ə]? the sound [ʊ]?

Mr. Jones wrote to his brother, Robert: "Would you like to come to the country with us on Sunday? We have a good cook and I think you'll have a good time and good food. I'll meet you at the bus."

Robert was a shy man. He did not like to cause trouble for others, but he came.

The bus arrived at seven o'clock on Saturday evening. Mr. and Mrs. Jones had had supper but Robert had not even had time for lunch, but he was too shy to say so.

"I had a good supper before I took the bus," he said. "I'm not hungry at all."

He was so tired from the bus ride that he slept late on Sunday morning.

"Don't forget to give Robert a good breakfast," Mrs. Jones told the cook. But the cook forgot and Robert was too shy to ask her.

At nine o'clock they drove to the country house and arrived there at one o'clock.

"We aren't going to eat until four o'clock because we had such a large breakfast, "Mr. Jones told Robert. "Would you like to go swimming?"

"No, I don't think so, "Robert said. "In fact, I don't feel very good. I haven't felt good for several hours."

"Perhaps you'd better see a doctor," Mr. Jones said. "I insist that you go to see one."

"I don't want to cause trouble," Robert said, but they went.

The doctor could not discover the trouble.

"The symptoms you have are sometimes the result of the wrong food,"the doctor said. "You'd better not eat much supper."

Robert was too weak to protest. The cook gave him some thin soup for supper.

He said goodbye to his brother at eight o'clock, and immediately ate two meals, one after the other, in a restaurant. While he ate, he wrote a note to thank his brother for the good time.

"I had fun," he wrote while he ate a second dessert. "You're lucky to have such a good cook. I shall never forget her meals."

Repeat aloud as much of the preceding narrative as you can remember.

4. Speed and rhythm drills

Read the following sentences with smooth sentence rhythm. Observe that the rhythm of the sentences in each group is similar.

a)  1.  Whát is he eáting?   A hám sándwich.
    2.  Whére is he góing?   To sée Jóhn.
    3.  Who is he meeting?   The two girls.
    4.  Whén is he cóming?   At twó thírty.

b)  1.  There's a lóng líne at the Státe Théater todáy.
    2.  We can meet John at séven thírty tomórrow.
    3.  It's a lóng wáy to Califórnia from hére.
    4.  It was tóo hót to pláy ténnis todáy.

c)  1.  The instrúctor gave us an assígnment.
    2.  Our bréakfast wasn't a very lárge one.
    3.  The assígnment wasn't a very lóng one.
    4.  The magazíne isn't a very góod one.

d)  1.  When he cáme I was tóo búsy to sée him.
    2.  Do you knów when the twó mén are cóming?
    3.  Did he ásk you when the bóy himsélf was góing?
    4.  When we ate, we made coffee enoúgh for áll of us.

5. Spelling

a) Spell the ING form of the following words.

              run              eat              come              meet

In what circumstances is a final consonant doubled to make the ING form of a verb?[1]

b) Spell the ING form of the following words.

              cry              lie              **try**              die

Form a rule for writing the ING form of words like the preceding ones.[2]

c) The instructor will dictate some of the following words. Spell them.

| running | eating | letting | meeting |
| coming | getting | living | putting |
| cutting | keeping | writing | riding |
| wishing | dying | lying | sleeping |
| cooking | raining | trying | writing |

d) Spell the past form of the following words.

              stop              wave              apply              enjoy

Form a rule for writing the past form of such words as the preceding.[3]

---

[1] Note to the teacher: The final consonant is doubled in the spelling when preceded by a single stressed vowel letter, (e.g., RUN, RUNNING but EAT, EATING).

[2] Before adding ING to words like DIE the IE is changed to Y (e.g., DIE, DYING).

[3] The final consonant is doubled before adding ED under the same circumnstances as for ING, (e.g., STOP, STOPPED): Final Y is changed to I before adding ED unless preceded by a vowel letter, (APPLY, APPLIED, but ENJOY, ENJOYED).

e) The instructor will dictate some of the following words. Spell them.

| getting | trying | stopped | heard |
| stopping | bearing | waved | enjoyed |
| waving | enjoying | applied | carried |
| applying | studying | obeyed | studied |
| obeying | | tried | cried |

## PRONUNCIATION

1. Drill on the recognition of sounds
2. The production of [e] and [i]
3. The production of [o] and [u]
4. Drill on verb terminations
5. Drill on stress and intonation
6. Speed drill - Government and
   Politics

## 1. Drill on the recognition of sounds

The instructor will pronounce the words in the following columns in any order he chooses. Indicate by number the words he pronounces.

|   | a | b | c |
|---|------|-------|-------|
| 1 | bed | song | shoe |
| 2 | bad | son | chew |
| 3 | beds | songs | shoes |
| 4 | bet | sung | chews |
| 5 | bets | sons | juice |
| 6 | bits | sunk | Jews |

Pronounce some of the words one column at a time. The instructor will indicate the word he hears.

## 2. The production of [e] and [i]

Read the following paragraphs with smooth sentence rhythm. Which words contain the sound [e]? the sound [i]?

This is the story of James who was always late because he was always sleepy during the day. He slept late in the morning. He was late for breakfast. He was late for classes. But he could never sleep in the evening. He always stayed awake until a late hour and read. During the day he was always sleepy. He used to sleep even in class.

"You shouldn't go to bed so late," his friends used to say.

"But I never feel sleepy at night," James always answered. "I only want to sleep during the day. I'd rather sleep than eat."

"You certainly need sleep," his friends agreed. "You even fall asleep during meals. Do you fall asleep while you're shaving?

"Frequently," James said.

His sleepiness didn't worry James especially, but he was worried about his examination.

"It's going to be an easy examination, probably," he confessed, "but I'm afraid that I am not going to stay awake. The effort of staying awake during the examination will probably put me to sleep."

On the day of the examination, James was very late. He had tried to go to sleep early on the evening before the examination, but he couldn't. He went to bed very late. During the examination he tried to stay awake, but he did not succeed. Half way through the ex-

187

amination he fell into a deep sleep.

"He looks so peaceful," the teacher said. "I don't like to wake him, but his grade, I'm afraid, is an E. But he looks so peaceful."

Repeat aloud as much of the preceding narrative as you can remember.

3. The production of [o] and [u]

Read the following paragraphs with smooth sentence rhythm. Which words contain the sound [o]? the sound [u]?

"I have a son," Mrs. Jones told me; "he is eight years old, and I don't know what to do with him. When I send him to school, he never goes, but he thinks of a lot of terrible things to do instead. For example, I sent him to school today, but I found him behind the barn at noon. He was very sick. He had tried to smoke.

"Do you know what he had done during the morning? I gave him a bowl of soup and twenty-five cents and sent him to school at eight o'clock. He didn't want to go, of course, but I told him he could have some ice cream when he came home, if he went to school. He went away from home very slowly.

"As soon as he left home, he went to a drug store and bought two sodas and some candy. When he left the drug store, he ate his soup and lost the bowl. Then he began to throw stones through windows and finally broke one. The window was Mrs. Howes' window. She telephoned me to tell me about it. I went out to look for my son.

"Before I could find him, he had removed his shoes and walked in a lot of water and made holes in his stockings. Then he tried to smoke. I found him behind the barn. He had hurt his foot and lost one of his shoes and he was very sick. I took him home and put him to bed in his room.

"Now, what am I going to do with him? Perhaps you think that it's funny, but I assure you that I don't consider it to be a good joke."

Repeat aloud as much of the preceding narrative as possible.

4. Drill on verb terminations

a) Pronounce the third person singular form of the present tense of the following words:

| a | b | c |
|---|---|---|
| touch | admit | live |
| change | avoid | call |
| arrange | last | copy |
| watch | profit | describe |
| criticize | waste | help |
| fix | affect | answer |
| raise | collect | believe |
| refuse | elect | control |
| publish | prevent | contain |
| arrange | subside | compare |
| brush | fit | improve |
| cash | suggest | lack |

| cause | depend | laugh |
| decrease | interpret | prescribe |
| discuss | count | prefer |
| express | end | resemble |
| increase | expect | shave |
| miss | insist | smile |
| recognize | invite | stay |

b) Pronounce the past form of the words in section (a)

## 5. Drill on stress and intonation

Read the following sentences with smooth sentence rhythm. Observe the stresses which have been indicated.

1. We ran out of bréad today.
2. They went óver the lesson in cláss.
3. They're going to look áfter the chíldren.
4. John doesn't get thróugh at six o'clóck.
5. I hópe you'll think it óver.
6. If you don't knów the word, look it úp in the díctionary.
7. The súit fitted so bádly that I had to take it báck.
8. How does he get alóng with the stúdents?
9. You'd better look oút for the cárs.
10. She ran ínto him in Detróit on Wédnesday.

## 6. Speed drill

Read the following paragraphs with smooth rhythm. Observe the stresses and pauses as indicated.

### Government and Politics

The most significant élement/ in the governmental organizátion/ of the United Státes/ is its émphasis/ upon the division of pówer.// Eách of the three bránches of góvernment,/ exécutive,/ législative,/ and judícial,/ has enough pówer/ to prevent abúses of power/ on the part of the óther branches;/ but no óne branch/ is powerful enough/ to succéed in a-buses of its ówn.//

The details of this system/ of checks and bálances/ are famíliar to citizens of demóc-racies,/ and the fúnction/ of eách of the three branches of góvernment/ in checking and balancing the óthers/ is álso well-known.//

The exécutive branch/ (the président and his cábinet)/ can check the législative branch/ (Cóngress)/ by the power of the véto.// The législative branch/ can check the exécutive branch/ by voting óver the veto.// The judícial branch/ (the Supreme Cóurt)/ can check bóth branches of góvernment/ by decláring an act unconstitútional.//

For many Américans,/ the most interesting súbject/ connected with góvernment/ is pólitics,/ although pólitics/ does not compríse/ as absórbing a part/ of daily lífe in the United States/ as it dóes/ in many óther countries.// Móst Americans/ are excited about pólitics/ for about a mónth before an eléction,/ when spéeches by political cándidates/ monopolize the rádio programs,/ and political tópics/ are prominent súbjects/ of news-paper héadlines and editórials.//

After the election, however,/ the excítement soon subsídes,/ and the attention of móst Americans/ turns to other subjects.// There are comparatively féw people/ in the United Státes/ (except those in governmental posítions)/ who maintain a víolent interest in polítics/ between eléctions.// Even for national elections/ it is unúsual/ for more than séventy percent of the voters/ to go to the pólls.//

People from óther countries/ are often surprísed/ to find such a comparative indífference/ to politics in the United Státes.// They are espécially surprised/ to find that college and university stúdents/ lack ínterest in politics./ and to find that in géneral,/ American wómen,/ who have had vóting privileges since 1919,/ neither know/ nor cáre very much about pólitics.//

The two major political groups/ in the United Státes/ are the Repúblican Party/ (symbolized in newspaper cartoons by the élephant)/ and the Democratic Party/ (symbolized by the donkey).// Other less próminent parties/ (for exámple,/ the Sócialist Party, the American Lábor Party/ and the Prohibítion Party)/ álso have candidates at eléction time;/ but nó candidate/ of any mínor party/ has yet been elécted/ to a prominent óffice/ in the national góvernment.//

Generalizátions/ concerning the classes of péople,/ theóries,/ and aíms/ which eách party represénts/ are difficult to máke.// For exámple,/ to say that the Repúblicans/ represent the búsiness man/ and the industrial Nórth/ while the Démocrats/ represent the fármer,/ the láborer,/ and the Sóuth,/ does not accóunt/ for the thóusands of Northern Démocrats/ and the Southern Repúblicans,/ or the Republican fármers.// In óther words,/ there is no définite list of characterístics/ for eíther party.//

Eléction day/ in the United Státes/ is the first Túesday/ after the first Mónday in Novémber.// Sometime befóre this date/ (frequently in Júne or July)/ representátives of each párty/ meet to choose the party's cándidates.// These méetings/ are called National Convéntions.// In addítion to these national convéntions,/ primary elections are held in sóme states/ in order to provide an opportúnity/ for the people of the státe/ to nominate cándidates.//

Memorize the first paragraph of this selection.

# LESSON XXXIV

## PRONUNCIATION

1. Drill on the recognition of sounds
2. The production of [a]
3. Dictation Exercise
4. Speed drill - Music in the United States

## 1. Drill on the recognition of sounds

The instructor will pronounce the words in the following columns in any order he chooses. Indicate by number the words he pronounces.

|   | a | b | c | d |
|---|---|---|---|---|
| 1 | bring | jest | vest | they |
| 2 | brim | yes | best | den |
| 3 | brims | just | a van | day |
| 4 | brings | joke | a ban | then |
| 5 | rings | yoke | a fan | ten |

Pronounce some of the words in the preceding columns, one column at a time. The instructor will indicate the words that he hears.

## 2. The production of [a]

Read the following paragraphs aloud. Which words contain the sound [a]?

Tom has a new job. He works at the hospital from eight o'clock until five o'clock. Last week he earned thirty dollars. It isn't a lot of money, but it's a lot for this job. His work consists of various things. Sometimes he copies records in the office. Sometimes he moves the cots in the wards. He always stops work at five o'clock sharp.

John's job isn't very good. He works at the hospital too, but he works outside all day. He has to help the gardener cut the grass. He also parks the cars of the visitors in the parking lot. This job is nice on a cool day, but it's hard on a hot day. Sometimes when all the cars are parked and the gardener isn't there, John can take a short nap in a nice cool spot.

When the boys got their first pay check Tom wanted to buy some new clothes. They walked several blocks to a sport shop and went in. Tom asked the clerk. "Does this shop stock spotted socks?" The clerk answered, "No sir, it does not, but it does stock a lot of sport socks." John and Tom looked at them and liked them very much. Together they bought a whole box of socks. They paid the clerk two dollars and went back to the hospital.

## 3. Dictation Exercise

Your teacher will dictate the following sentences at normal conversational speed.[1] Write them on a piece of paper.

1. Mary called up Ruth
2. "Please come over to see me this afternoon."
3. Ruth put on her new brown suit and left the house.

---

[1] Note to the teacher: This exercise is to give the students practice in hearing the second part of the two word expressions such as CALL UP, COME OVER, etc. Read the sentences at normal speed and without special emphasis on the two word expressions.

191

4. She got on the bus at the corner.
5. When she arrived at Hill Street she got off.
6. Mary was making coffee when Ruth arrived.
7. "I'm sorry, but we ran out of sugar today," said Mary.
8. "I can get along without it," Ruth said.
9. Afterwards, the girls washed the dishes and put them away.
10. Mary and Ruth get along well with each other.

4. Speed drill

Read the following paragraphs with smooth rhythm. Observe the stresses and pauses as indicated.

### Music in the United States

Like the histories of other arts/ in the United States,/ the history of músic/ is bríef.// It is nécessary/ to state agáin/ that the people of the éarly eras/ were práctical people,/ búsy with problems of survíval,/ and not recéptive to artistic actívity.// Even áfter the United Státes/ had aquíred a national góvernment/ and some degree of secúrity,/ it was éasier/ to use ready-made musical ímports/ than to create a nátive product.//

There was no important compóser/ in the United States/ before the nínettenth céntury.// When tálented composers finally díd develop,/ they were unáble/ to get ádequate musical traíning/ in the United Státes;/ cónsequently,/ the fírst composers/ spent many yéars/ in the musical cénters of Europe,/ where they acquíred/ a natural admirátion/ for European techníque/ and European súbjects.// The music of these fírst composers,/ thérefore,/ was not characteristically Américan.//

Láter composers,/ for exámple,/ Edward McDówell,/ H.F. Gílbert,/ and C.W. Cádman,/ looked for nátive thémes/ in Índian music and negro spírituals.// Many óthers/ have found inspiration in jázz.//

Since vísitors from other countries/ know more about jazz/ than about óther developments/ in the music of the United Státes,/ little will be said hére/ about this significant súbject,/ except to méntion/ the outstanding contribútion of George Gérshwin,/ who has transférred the values of jázz/ to "sérious" music.//

Próminent fígures in musical hístory/ whose names are less famíliar to vísitors/ are Aaron Cópland,/ Deems Táylor,/ Roy Hárris,/ and William Schúman.//

Although many Américans/enjóy imported operatic composítions,/ and although radio broadcasts/ of ópera programs are pópular,/ ópera has never been a very successful fórm/ o f native musical expréssion/ in the United Státes.// Gershwin's fólk-opera,/ "Porgy and Béss," is an outstanding excéption.// In the field of líght opera,/ howéver,/there are many pópular compósers,/ for exámple,/ Victor Hérbert,/ Reginald De Kóven,/ Sigmund Rómberg,/ Jerome Kérn,/ and Irving Berlín.//

A few contémporary singers/ deserve special méntion.// Perhaps the most ínteresting/ are the negro singers,/ Marían Ánderson,/ Dorothy Máynor,/ Roland Háyes,/ and others.// The people of the United Státes/ are still impréssed by foreign námes,/ and many nátive musical ártists/ assume Européan names/ because of the popular impréssion/ that impórted musician are bést.//

Although the United Státes/ has not yet reáched musical matúrity,/ there have beén/ at least two' important indicátions of grówth/ during the twentieth céntury:/ fírst,/ the development of/ and émphasis upon/ music education in the public schools;/ and, second,/ the rise of the symphony orchestra.//

During the past fifteen years/ American educators/ have recognized the need/ for an increased appreciation of fine music.// With the new leisure/ provided by industrial-izátion,/ there is opportunity/ for aesthetic actívity.// The schools/ are therefore at-tempting/ to encourage musically talented students/ to develop their talents.// Courses in vocal and instrumental music/ have become a significant part/ of the school curricu-lum;/ orchestras,/ bands,/ and choruses,/ supervised by trained teachers,/ are stimu-late participation/ in musical activities.//

Moreover,/ music educátion/ is not confined to the talented.// Stúdents/ who lack the ability/ to partícipate in orchestras or chóruses/ are acquiring a táste for fine music/ through coúrses in music appreciátion.//

A second indication/ of increasing ínterest in músic/is the rise of the symphony ór-chestra,// Since 1842,/ when the Philharmonic Socíety of New Yórk was estáblished,/ the number of symphony órchestras/ has incréased to more than fífty.// These fífty/ include some of the fínest/ instrumental organizations in the wórld.// The orchestras of síx cít-ies,/ New Yórk,/ Philadélphia,/ Bóston,/ Chicágo,/ Minneápolis,/ and Cleveland,/ are especially prominent;/ but even comparatively small cities/ have ambítious and cápable symphony orchestras.//

There are three ways/ of listening to symphony órchestras/ in the United Státes:/ one can attend cóncerts/ in city auditóriums or on university cámpuses;/ one can lísten/ to the radio broadcasts of these cóncerts;/ or one can obtain recórdings/ of musical com-positions/ played by the best symphony órchestras/ in the coúntry.// The tremendous íncrease/ in the sale of symphony récords/ during the past ten yéars/ indicates a rapidly growing appreciátion/ of fine music in the United Státes.//

Memorize the first paragraph of this selection.

## PRONUNCIATION

1. The consonant combination [n-ð]
2. Drill on the pronunciation of cognate words
3. Dictation Exercise
4. Speed drill - Religion in the United States

## 1. The consonant combination [n-ð]

Pronounce the following phrase.

in the city

The consonant combination [n-ð] - in the - is extremely common in English. In this combination the [n] is pronounced with the tongue in the position for [ð]. The nasal passage opens for [n] and closes for [ð].

Practice the following sounds in rapid succession.

[ n - ð - n - ð - n - ð - n - ð - n - ð ]

Pronounce the following phrases.

| | |
|---|---|
| in the house | It's in the house. |
| on the table | It's on the table. |
| in their room | It's in their room. |
| on their street | It's on their street. |
| on the desk | It's on the desk. |
| in the letter | It's in the letter. |
| in the book | It's in the book. |
| on the chair | It's on the chair. |

Pronounce the following phrase.

the boy and the girl             [ðə bɔɪ ən ðə gərl]

Notice that the word and is pronounced [ən]. The combination [n-ð] - and the - is pronounced with the tongue in the same position. Only the nasal passage opens and closes.
Practice the following phrases

the boy and the girl
the man and the woman
the book and the pencil
the question and the answer

now and then
here and there

they came and they went
they walked and they talked

## 2. Drill on the pronunciation of cognate words

Pronounce the following cognate words.

| | | |
|---|---|---|
| circular | confusion | activity |
| superior | provision | vanity |

194

| realize | decision | formality |
| organize | ambition | regularity |
| recognize | production | variety |
| comprehend | condition | convenient |
| ignore | future | sympathetic |
| consult | actual | numerous |
| protect | natural | religious |

## 3. Dictation Exercise

Your teacher will dictate the following sentences at normal conversational speed.[1] Write them on a piece of paper.

1. The boys called up their girl friends.
2. They wanted to make dates for the week-end.
3. Robert and John asked Mary and Anna to go on a picnic.
4. James and David asked Ruth and Barbara to go to the movies.
5. All the boys get along well together.
6. They all like movies.
7. They all like picnics.
8. David has a car, and he invited them all to go to the movies on Friday night.
9. John also has a car, and he invited them all to go on a picnic Saturday afternoon.
10. They finally decided to go together to the movies and the picnic.

## 4. Speed drill

Read the following paragraphs with smooth rhythm. Observe the stresses and pauses as indicated.

### Religion in the United States

Knówledge of a few fácts/ about the religious hístory/ of the United Státes/ is important for vísitors/ who want to understand the cóuntry.// The United Státes/ is predominantly Prótestant/ because the earliest séttlers/ came from Éngland,/ a Prótestant country,/ and because for many generátions/ most of the immigrants/ came from óther Protestant countries/ in northern Éurope,/ especially from Hólland,/ Gérmany,/ Scótland/ and Swéden.//

The fírst colonists/ came to this part of the New Wórld/ for relígious and económic reasons.// Mány of them were dissátisfied/ with their life in Éngland/ and they were especially dissatisfied/ with the religious restríctions/ which would not let them wórship/ as they wíshed.// People who crossed the Atlántic/ for relígious reasons/ díd so/ because their religious belíefs/ were dífferent from thóse/ of the offícial state chúrch.//

Mémbers of one religious gróup/ usually lived togéther/ in the same cólony;// there were Púritans/ in Massachusetts Báy Colony,/ Báptists/ in Rhode Ísland,/ Quákers/ in Pennsylvánia,/ Roman Cátholics/ in Máryland,/ etc.//

Naturally,/ people whose religious belíef/ was stróng enough/ to make them cross an ócean/ were so enthusiástic about that belíef/ that they wanted óther people to sháre it.// The sáme people/ who had objécted/ to religious dictátorships in Éngland/ tried to es-

---

[1]Note to the teacher: This exercise is to give the students practice in hearing the past forms of the verbs. Read at normal speed without special emphasis on the past forms.

tablish new dictatorships/ of their own.// When conflicts/ about religious policies arose,/ dissenting groups/ separated from the main colony,/ moved away to a new location,/ and began another organization/ which sometimes became as intolerant/ as that against which it had protested.//

An important result/ of the first political and religious dictatorships,/ and of the reaction against these dictatorships,/ was the separation of the church and the state.// One of the statements/ in the Constitution of the United States declares, / "Congress shall make no law/ respecting an establishment of religion,/ or prohibiting the free exercise thereof."// There has never been/ a state church in this country;/ and when any religion group is attacked,/ most other religious groups insist/ that the principle of religious freedom/ should be defended.//

A conspicuous and important result/of religious freedom/ is the variety of religious organizations in the United States.// Immigrants/ who have come from all parts of the world/ have brought their religious beliefs with them;/ and still other organizations/ have originated in this country.// The latest census figures/ report 256 religious sects in the United States/with a total of 55,000,000 members/ (more than one-third/ of the population of the country).//

The many denominations/ which comprise Protestantism in the United States/ are separate organizations/ based on the beliefs of the man/ that founded them.// Many present-day members/ of Protestant denominations/ do not agree/ with the founders of their denominations/ regarding specific doctrines,/ but the denominations continue to exist/ under the same names.// A few of the largest/ are Presbyterian,/ Baptist,/ Methodist,/ Episcopal,/ and Lutheran.//

Before the days of automobiles and movies,/ the church was the center of community life.// Parties,/ suppers,/ and "socials"/ were popular forms of community entertainment.// Churches still provide these,/ but their popularity/ has declined a great deal/ during an era of more sophisticated entertainment.//

Practice the pronunciation of the following words.

| | | | |
|---|---|---|---|
| Baptist | location | attack | conspicuous |
| belief | Lutheran | comprise | dissatisfied |
| census | Methodist | cross | dissenting |
| colonist | policy | decline | enthusiastic |
| colony | Presbyterian | defend | intolerant |
| conflict | principle | move away | official |
| denomination | Protestant | object to | religious |
| dictatorship | Puritan | originate | sophisticated |
| doctrine | Quaker | prohibit | specific |
| Episcopal | religion | protest | |
| era | Roman Catholic | separate from | |
| freedom | Scotland | | |
| generation | sect | | |
| Germany | Sweden | | |
| Holland | variety | | |
| immigrant | | | |

Memorize the first paragraph of this selection.